The
AFFAIRS
of
MEN

The
AFFAIRS
of
MEN

Harvey E. Kaye, M.D.

A Tom Doherty Associates Book

New York

THE AFFAIRS OF MEN

Book design by Heidi Eriksen

A Forge Book
Published by Tom Doherty Associates, LLC
175 Fifth Avenue
New York, NY 10010

www.tor.com

Forge® is a registered trademark of Tom Doherty Associates, LLC.

Library of Congress Cataloging-in-Publication Data

Kaye, Harvey E.
    The affairs of men / Harvey E. Kaye.
        p. cm.
    "A Tom Doherty Associates book."
    ISBN 0-312-87897-4 (hc)
    ISBN 0-765-30021-4 (pbk)
    1. Men—Psychology. 2. Men—Social conditions 3. Masculinity. I. Title.

HQ1090 .K38 2001
305.31—dc21   2001023600

First Hardcover Edition: June 2001
First Trade Paperback Edition: June 2002

Printed in the United States of America

0 9 8 7 6 5 4 3 2 1

To
TERRY, the best of wives
TED and ELLIE RUBIN, the best of friends

Acknowledgments

My career in psychiatry has provided access to several thousand minds of men and women: their feelings, fantasies, and dreams, along with the realities of their lives. Without that unique experience provided by them, this book would never have been written.

I applaud the contributions of Ms. Melissa Ann Singer via her editing, of Mr. Harold Roth via his agenting, and of my colleague, Theodore I. Rubin, M.D., via his amiable hectoring.

It is hoped that observations made and opinions advanced will serve to stimulate thought and controversy. The responsibility for them is solely mine, and the aforementioned trinity should not be castigated for them.

Contents

The
AFFAIRS
of
MEN

1

The Masculine Mystique

Imagine the discovery of a new drug, a sovereign remedy with horrendous social import. Let's call it the "Reality Inducer." While the usual narcotics induce varied states of sensate anarchy, the Reality Inducer would create a psychic world devoid of illusion. One who ingests would see things as they are, rather than as one has been programmed to see them. It would induce a condition of compassionate detachment in which distortion, myth, and false coloration would be stripped away from reality. Obviously this elixir should not be marketed, lest our social fabric be ripped to shreds. What would happen to the speeches of the politicians, the protestations of lovers, and concepts like honor and heroism, cowardice and martyrdom? How much of our behavior and how many of our beliefs are founded upon individual and collective delusion? But join me in a fanciful dose. Let us relax in its unique effects and contemplate the minds of men.

When Aristotle defined man as a "rational animal," he was being charitable. Men's minds have an outer crust of reason, surrounding a molten core of archaic residues, primordial passions, mythologic themes, and inchoate drives and fantasies. A man's perception of himself and his world is filtered through and altered by this center. The core is conceptualized as the "unconscious" by the psychologically oriented, or as the subcortical centers of the brain and biochemical substrate by the more physiologically minded. Rage and sexual responses can be localized in areas of the brain far beneath the cerebral cortex, the rind of the brain in which the rational processing occurs. However, the manner and type of the reaction are determined by the individual's previous experiences.

The Unconscious, functioning in part as a unique recorder, incorporates within itself previous unremembered experiences, repressed memories, and the unrecognized training to which it has been exposed by parental and other critical figures. These impressions are frequently distorted by inaccuracies, the prejudices and expectations of others, and the exigencies and circumstances of the child's life situation. The Reality Inducer is designed to dispel these distortions and illusions. And nowhere are they more apparent than in the male's conception of his masculinity.

Civilization has created a Masculine Mystique, a complex of quasi-mystical attitudes and expectations surrounding the male in his society. Utilizing parents, peers, and cultural institutions, already unwittingly infected by it, the Mystique softly and subtly insinuates its siren song into the recording apparatus of each man as he develops, luring him from the facts of his maleness to the outer reaches of exaggeration, caricature, and illusion, and finally, at times, to self-destruction. The aura of the Mystique penetrates the essence of a man's existence. Permeating his physical apparatus, his psychological set, and his social interactions, the melody seduces man from what he is, and offers instead a grandiose image all but impossible to live up to and still remain human.

During the birth process, the infant's head descends from the mother's pelvis flexed on its breastbone. Rotating inward, extending, restituting, and finally turning outward, the head greets the outside world, followed by his shoulders and the remainder of its tiny form. The obstetrician, having breathed a sigh of relief that there was no umbilical cord constricting the neck, confidently grasps the child by the feet, slaps the soles, and is rewarded by the cry which the new mother will find maternally inspiring, and later occasionally maddening. A cursory examination of the pubic area reveals the presence of a penis, and the exhausted mother and nail-biting father are informed that they have a son. From that moment, the cultural indoctrination begins.

The blue blanket, the miniature boxing gloves, the Superman costume, the toy guns and fire engines, all subtly inform this newly hatched bit of protoplasm of the great and impossible expectations which will be within the core of his recently acquired humanity. He is to become the embodiment of heroism and courage, aggressivity and aptitude, an amalgam of the fantasies of Hemingway and Mailer. The roughhouse play with adults, the injunction that "little boys don't cry," the "did you win?" when he returns after his first pugilistic encounter, nose bloodied and tears only barely contained: the message is received, the boy is trained to be a "man." Vulnerability is a vice, emotionality is odious, and stoicism connotes strength.

Unwitting conspirators, parents and society weave the Mystique into the psyche of the developing boy. The seductive promise of limitless potentials proves irresistible. A spirited marlin rising to the bait, the tad swallows the Neanderthal Ideal, the image of the conquering male, clad in the skins of animals slain in single-handed combat, dragging the woman, his mother, or some reasonable facsimile into his cave. In his dreams and fantasies, he has faced the paternal dragon. Despite his dread of castration or annihilation, he has survived, penis intact, taller and broader in body and spirit. He might now envision himself a Lancelot who has imaginatively dabbled with Guinevere, while a benign and understanding Arthur has stood patiently by, restrained by the wisdom of a Merlin or a Dr. Spock.

Spurred by the insistent flow of testosterone, with its resultant increase in aggressivity and physical growth, a boy's marriage to the Mystique is further cemented. Through his rearing, his training in school, and the attitudes of the women he encounters, our young knight is encouraged to further flex his musculature. In the good old days, so much of this was symbolic. Differentiating himself from "the frail sex," he would gallantly offer them his seat on a bus, carry their school books, and pick up the tab at the local soda fountain. As our society has "advanced" however, this is increasingly acted out instead by joining

gangs, referring to women as "hos," and throwing "moth-
erfucker" around with bravado and careless abandon. Con-
formity to the Mystique rapidly becomes a measure of
manhood, a thermometer of "masculinity." Again, little
boys or big men don't cry. Instead they are to become the
image of John Wayne, walking down the streets of Laredo
or Saigon, with catlike mincing steps and swaggering hips,
ready and able to deal with any adversity without the shed-
ding of a groan or a tear.

Following the puberty rite of his particular culture, be
it confirmation, bar mitzvah, or a vest impregnated with
live wasps placed upon his chest, the boy theoretically enters "manhood," with all the "privileges" accorded to the
Achiever. Regardless of economic conditions or physical
limitations, he is to return with the spoils of the hunt, or
suffer the loss of self-esteem. He is to attain status and
prestige, and transfer these to his family, in a society that
has precious little status and prestige to bestow. Furthermore, our Achiever is expected to assume ill-defined responsibilities and to cope effectively with them. His
legendary sexual prowess is awesome. Expected to produce
an erection on demand, and to insistently and everlastingly
satisfy his mate, the man must become a sexual athlete.
Impotence or infertility equals personal inadequacy. Finally, he must present the appearance of independence in
a society predicated on a complex of mutual interdepen-
dencies.

Like creativity and rumor, the Masculine Mystique is
difficult to delineate. However, recurring themes in dreams,
fantasies, actions, and aspirations of men define certain con-

stellations around which it settles. These by no means define its limits, but they will serve as representative illustrations of its manifestations.

The Superman Syndrome

Superman has been embedded in the recesses of men's minds for thousands of years. The image of an indestructible being, all-powerful and victorious, has persisted from the anthropomorphic deities of prehistoric times, from the Grecian Zeus, the Teutonic Wotan, the Aztec Quetzalcoatl, to our more contemporary Promethean figures. It has currently emerged among the demigods created by our culture of celebrity, and may best be observed in the Olympian heights of the athlete and the entertainer, and in the depths of the Faustian partnership between the advertising and media enterprises.

Human beings seem prone to feel a "lack"—a lack of importance, significance, control of their destinies, et cetera, and are all too ready to identify with proxy figures that they create to serve as their surrogates. Men, after all, did create gods in their own images. In place of the stars in the heavens, they have fashioned stars on Earth, and have positioned them on athletic fields, motion picture screens, in newspapers and magazines, and have regarded them with awe.

Consider the psyche of the rabid fan of a professional ball club (baseball, football, basketball, soccer). He designates "his" team as his alter ego, even though the players are merely highly paid alien journeymen who skip from team to team with remarkable agility at the drop of a dollar (the average basketballer earns $3.5 million, and the baseballer pockets $2 million, while the professional football player must content himself with a mere $1.5 million per year). One quarter of a billion dollars for ten years of shortstopping, while the Yankees pay a pitcher the equivalent of $3,000 per pitch. Yet the fans continue their wild applause and subsidization even though the price of a seat in the upper deck in Yankee Stadium has increased by more than 25 percent, from $26 to $33 in the past year. Why? Do they see their stellar surrogates twinkling all the brighter if they up the ante? Or sympathize with their beloved "home team," a corporate entity concerned only with the bottom line à la Disney, which will rapidly relocate its franchise to the town that will provide the newest stadium to milk the maximum from its fans, who can no longer pay the inflated prices at the ticket window or refreshment stand? The fan identifies so strongly with the players that his testosterone level rises along with theirs, and remains high after the victory, resulting in soccer fans killing each other at the end of a match. The loser, with plummeting testosterone, slinks into some darkened corner of some seedy bar, not to be heard from again until the next game. The barrier between the Supermen on the field and the poor souls in the stands has dissolved, for better or worse. Journalism slavishly cooperates. The front page of the *New York Times* of April 16, 2000, featured the bulletin that "Cal Ripken, Jr., hitting his third single of the night, became the 24th [*sic*] major league baseball player to accumulate 3,000 hits." A bulletin of such magnitude pushed stories of stalled flood relief in Venezuela, the failure of the diplomatic quarantine of Yugoslavia, and other trivia to the back pages.

The stars seen on the silver screen are presented, literally and figuratively, in larger-than-life proportions. William Goldman, a screenwriter of Oscar proportions, in his book *Which Lie Did I Tell?* advises future screenwriters as follows: "Stars do not—repeat—do not play heros—stars play gods. And your job as a screenwriter is to genuflect, if you are lucky enough to have them glance in your direction." Imagine Leonardo DiCaprio, of puerile features and questionable intellect, as the chairman of Earth Day 2000, and interviewing the president of the United States on the problems of Earth! And the president acting as coconspirator! How bizarre can it get??? John Wayne, Superman of the westerns, is reported to have disliked riding horses, innumerable supersex symbols were same-sex oriented, and one can, of course, go on and on with innumerable misreprepresentations manufactured by studios, their PR people, the stars' PR representatives, but, most of all, by the fantasies of their fans. Consider the astronomical prices paid at auction for inconsequential memorabilia from one ex-star or another. Why do their fans have to physically touch them, get an autograph or a wisp of their clothing? Recall the ceiling of the Sistine Chapel, in which God's finger nearly touches Adam's, and reflect on the similarities. Is the godhead physically transferred from the deity to the acolyte?

The media need advertising and vice versa; ergo the formation of an unholy alliance, with each contributing to the conning of America. Michael Jordan, the Superman dubbed "His Airness" by the media, was an extremely talented player of basketball with a winning personality, who earned 35 to 50 million dollars per year simply by lending his name to products that were not only out of the financial reach of many of his adoring fans, but were perceived as worth killing for by some of them. Tiger Woods is a walking advertisement for Nike, Andre Agassi hawks razor blades and cameras, while Arnold Palmer, who had an army of fans devoted to him, pitches tires on the radio. Larry King, TV pitchman extraordinaire, endorses so many health food products, which are to be ingested each day, that one wonders how any stomach can accommodate them in a twenty-four-hour span.

Men are swamped by the multiplicity of idealized images instructing them as to what to purchase, what to feel, whom to vote for, and how to live their lives. The Mystique, with its imperative of the superlative, makes its contribution. So many men are blinded by the Mystique's utilization of the manufactured Superimages that dispassionate rationality is too often put on hold.

The media, in collusion with the Mystique, promotes the nonsensicality produced by the endorsers, who exploit the Superman-fan relationship. The real Superman never would have done it.

The Sexual Athlete

The Mystique has encouraged what Freud's biographer, Ernest Jones, referred to as "an unduly phallocentric view" of sexuality in our culture. Man, the primate with the largest penis, is too frequently regarded as a phallus with a body attached as an addendum. Seizing upon the obvious fact that the male has a projecting appendage that must be actively inserted into a female, the Mystique has, at times, deified it, endowed it with magical powers, and expected men to live up to this glorious exaltation. The male member has consequently been regarded as majestic, while the woman's pudendum—"(1) from the Latin: something to be ashamed of; (2) the external genitals of the female, vulva"— has been accorded second-class citizenship. Dreams of towering steeples, racing automobiles, and spaceships blasting off may be penile representations, while purses and vases may represent the vagina. The fact that a woman's sexual apparatus has greater orgastic potential than the male's is only now coming to light after thousands of years, and is causing the Mystique considerable concern.

In dreams, the size of a person or object is frequently an indication of its importance or power to the dreamer. To a child, the size of his parents and other adults is itself indicative of their importance and strength. A young boy is awed by the size of his father's phallus, and aspires to reach the same proportions. Similarly, the size of the penis is often equated with a man's virility. The equation states that the massiveness of the penis is in direct proportion to the virility of its possessor. Since all but a very few men have approximately the same erect penile size, and many feel their organs to be abnormally small, something is obviously amiss. The problem is that men ofttimes focus their feelings of masculine inadequacy onto their penises. An illustration of this concerns one particular segment of the homosexual community, the members of which compulsively journey from one public toilet to the next, seeking encounters with a penis larger than their own. They have their trousers tailored to accentuate a genital bulge, producing a modernized version of the codpiece of yore. Comparisons are made nightly at gay bars and baths. The unconscious wish is to magically incorporate the other man's virility, via fellatio or anal intercourse, or, at the least, to neutralize the other man's presumptive superior masculinity. This fruitless and unending quest is both poignant and pointless. They never win: the next one may be bigger.

The male's procreative powers have been so touchy a subject that the Mystique has averted its eyes, and allowed men to assume that the "infertile couple" was synonymous with "the barren wife." That 30 to 50 percent of infertile couples are childless due to some difficulty in the male has been a well-kept secret that is only recently being confronted. The male takes the credit for the pregnancy. The "proud father" is hailed. How frequently does one hear of the "proud mother"? He passes out cigars symbolic of his productive penis. When he doesn't produce, no cigars. Potentates divorce spouses who give birth only to daughters, despite the fact that it is basically the sperm which determines the sex of the offspring. The infertile male feels unvirile, although the production of sperm and the manufacture of the virilizing testosterone are two separate functions of the testicles. An obstetrical paper on the medical workup of the infertile male cautioned: "The man should be approached with delicacy, interest, and optimism. Careful explanation should be given that the semen quality is in no way related to his ability to perform as a male. Often, telling a man that he is the cause of the infertility problem may be a severe blow to his pride." I have never read such a delicate approach advised in the fertility workup of a woman. Male fragility in matters procreative is brittle indeed.

It is in the game of Performance that the Mystique reaches its apotheosis, for the man is truly expected to be a Sexual Athlete. For the moment, let's put aside the fact that recent studies indicate that more than 30 percent of men are either relatively disinterested or dissatisfied with sex. Let's even table the fact that at least 40 percent of men over sixty have erectile problems to a significant degree. Nonetheless, the male is conceptualized as an insatiate satyr, prancing around in a state of perpetual erection, able to perform under any and all circumstances, and lecherously enlarging at the drop of a handkerchief or the rise of a hemline. Impotency is not only unthinkable, it is unmentionable, although, as noted, it is by no means uncommon, and appears to be on the rise. Regardless of the level of the woman's arousal and lubricity, the male is expected to satisfy. He must maintain his erection and restrain his ejaculation until she attains her requisite degree of orgastic ecstasy. Should he "come" too soon or too late, if he misses that moment of simultaneity, he has played poorly, and may be benched. With women increasingly regarding their climax as a "right," and since the insertor is deemed the responsible agent for the attainment of this right, orgastic failure in a woman is looked upon, by her mate, as a denial by him of her constitutional prerogative. But, pathetically, even if she murmurs, "Honey, it's me, not you," he doesn't believe her.

Heroically, science is endeavoring to come to the aid of the beseiged male with its bountiful production of Viagra and synthetic testosterone. The problem to date is that testosterone increases the desire but does little for the performance, while Viagra enhances the performance, but not necessarily the desire. But more of this in later chapters. Some deus ex machina will descend from the heavens to rescue the male member.

The Neanderthal Ideal

First, a few words of apology to the Neanderthal. Our cultural stereotype portrays this 75,000-year-old Stone Age humanoid as the personification of brawn: a muscular and hirsute individual who lived by strength alone, dragging his women into caves by their hair, and bashing his neighbor's skull with his massive club. He may well have been simply an embattled soul, too busy with the essentials of survival to be overly concerned with such superfluities as warfare, rape, and other leisure activities. I see no reason to assume that he was incapable of intelligence, warmth, and affection. But the Mystique feeds on stereotypes, and we must meet it on its own terms.

The Neanderthal Ideal is a reversion to the primitive. The complexities of life, with their tortuous alternatives, are simply solved by the rejection of the rational, and the evocation of the physical. When dispute arises, punch if individual, war if national. In man's struggle between the sinew and the sensible, the former too frequently emerges on top. The specter of the male as the physical brute, the ruthless and violent hunter and warrior, emerges as the symbol of "virility."

Bethesda Fountain is a picturesque oasis in the middle of Central Park. On Sundays, New York weather permitting, it attracts hordes of humanity. Expressively attired in what they view as their individual "thing," a multitude of egos enact their conceptualized self-images on this massive stage. Strolling troubadours, strumming guitarists, and bongo bands beating with primitive rhythmicity provide the musical background for the spectacle. The outfits often display the people as they would like to see themselves, and the costumes are varied. One striking motif is the portrayal of brawn: the motorcycle cultists, their jackets unsleeved, exhibit their biceps and deltoids; those decked out in headbands and other Indian paraphernalia recall the "noble savage." The Neanderthal comes alive in New York City. Invite the fantasy, it seldom refuses an invitation.

The adulation of the primitive is not confined to the fountain and its visitors, nor to our time and place. The elaboration of the fifteenth- and sixteenth-century codpiece, the padded shoulders of men's jackets, the rugged square-jaw hero of romantic novels, and the exaggerated simian gait of swaggering adolescents are all extensions of the Neanderthal Ideal. It is also blatantly obvious among the Mister Americas on Muscle Beach.

The Neanderthal Ideal is rooted in our racial and individual histories. During the evolutionary and historical descent of *Homo sapiens*, conditions for survival dictated the development of various qualities in the male that more effectively ensured the survival of both the individual and his species. In earlier times, the struggle for mere physical existence placed a premium upon the acquisition of a substantial musculature and supporting skeletal structure to enable the man to hunt, to defend himself and his clan from predators, and to aggress when conditions warranted it. While his developing intelligence, language skills, and tool utilization placed him somewhat apart from other animals, the need for physical strength was obvious. The fact that the male was approximately 40 percent more powerful physically than the female placed the onus of more arduous muscular labors upon him. Moreover, he was fleeter of foot and more physiologically prepared for aggressive behavior than was his mate. It is a fair assumption that when humankind progressed from a nomadic to a more settled existence, the males hewed the forest for timber, while the females prepared the home; and that men killed for skins, while the women made the clothing from them. Again, brawn was the sine qua non for the male, and was naturally imbedded in the hard drive of the Mystique.

In a world in which the force necessary to push a button or to press on an accelerator is the requisite strength needed for survival, men still perceive of themselves as muscular madcaps, divinely ordained to perform feats of might. For example, witness the spectacular rise in interest in, and fanaticism for, professional wrestling, both in the arenas and on television. The more garish the costumed participant, the louder the groans, the dirtier the tactics, the more the fans scream in appreciation. For goodness' sake, if this isn't an explosion of the Neanderthal at the end of this millennium, what is!

Presented with guns as playthings, a street lore that sanctifies the "victor," movie and television idols who heartily partake in violence, a boy can't prevent the attributes of the Neanderthal from sinking deeper into his developing psyche. As he ages, he sees girls ogling shoulder-padded football heroes, and is taught that economic success is predicated on "making it," and riding roughshod over one's competitor. Visions of the caveman reemerge in new contexts. The examples are numerous but the phantasm remains the same. There are alternatives. In societies more oriented to the Confucian ideals, for example, unnecessary violence and gut-piercing competitiveness are shunned. Criminality and social irresponsibility, excessive ego-centeredness and lack of cooperativeness, are deemed shameful. But our society, at present, does not seem to be geared for any rapid turnaround. But let us hope that the Neanderthal remains no more than some aberrant relic, rather than a future actuality.

The Achiever Complex

Ever since Eve's fraternization with the serpent and her appetite for apples caused mankind's ouster from Eden, man has had to exert himself in the cause of providing sustenance for his, and his family's, survival. The Mystique, however, is seldom satisfied with the basics. Extrapolating from life's labors, it has devised the concept of the

Achiever, the accumulator of status and prestige that rank a man as "worthwhile" or "important," or something other than a wastrel or a bum. No longer is the fact of labor sufficient. The type of work, along with its various fringe benefits, provide a seldom-to-be-satiated goal, the nebulous measure of a man. How can a man look at his image in the mirror while shaving morning after morning, without seeing his golden parachute enveloping him in a halo, and still retain his self-respect? To further complicate this absurdity, the Mystique has ordained that not only is a man judged by his status accumulation, but his family is to be judged by his performance. Temptingly it whispers: "More, you owe it to yourself. More, you owe it to them."

The scramble for achievement is primarily found in the upwardly mobile middle class. The lowest on the socioeconomic scale ofttimes see the climb as too unreachably high, with the odds significantly stacked against them. Their own social group may actively discourage their attempts, i.e., by deriding attempts at academic excellence. Those at the top have no appreciable gains to make, unless they delight in playing one-upmanship with their peers. But those in the vast middle strive. They catch glimpses of the jackpot in the sky, and are the most vulnerable to a fall. Urged on by a work ethic that trumpets, "Work is beautiful, and the more you work the more beautiful you become," they strain for the higher house on the hill, the more prestigious job, and the more expensively attired woman. The legendary second trophy wife, exhibited by the Achiever, has brought looks of admiration to some, and profound misery to others. The symbols of achievement become the goal, rather than the enjoyment of their gains.

Men happy with their work as teachers are urged to become principals; brilliant medical clinicians and researchers are pushed into the role of departmental administrators; artists become commercial hacks; and reasonably contented workers rise to be alienated foremen, neither blue-collar nor management, and under continuous stress. To remain on a comfortable level is seen as somewhat sinful, and those pushed to "advance" too often advance to an unhappy state. They can take solace from their enhanced status or console themselves with that extra martini or two, or three, or four.

Since the Achiever Complex grows fastest in the vocational medium, the other areas of a man's life suffer. The Achiever becomes the tired husband or absentee father. The tragic image of the Japanese "salaryman" who is so welded to his job that he seldom sees his wife or children, and finds himself estranged from them after he retires, is a poignant figure. With the work week of a self-employed person averaging some fifty-five hours, moments of leisure are few, and are apt to be contaminated by feelings of guilt, since funtime does not feel productive.

The Achiever Complex begins in the cradle and ends in the grave. In our society, achieving is as endemic as is water to a fish in a fish tank. It's so ubiquitous that one takes it for granted. But, again, the family does inject its additional contribution. The competition between mothers as to whose child sat up first, uttered "mama" earliest, et cetera, is sometimes fearsome to behold. All too often the child is seen as an extension of the parental egos, and is expected to achieve that which they had coveted for themselves so they can bask in the reflected glory of their child's

attainments. The excitement and wonderment of the educational experience becomes of secondary importance to the
superior grade on the report card. As the boy becomes the
man, he must confront the American Dream of two cars in
every garage, and so much the better if one is a Porsche
and the other a Mercedes. He is even urged to contemplate
his own death: the type of funeral, the height and decor of
the tombstone, or the size of the mausoleum. Once again,
for the last time, the question is posed: "How much land
does a man need?"

I do not mean to imply that achievement per se is suspect or pathological. There is genuine joy in mastery and
excitation in expanding one's domain, talents, and capabil-
ities. These are personal additives that broaden the scope
and depth of one's life. But I do inveigh against the obsession with achieving and the compulsion to accumulate
status and prestige at the expense of the remainder of one's
personality and life. It is this neurotic imbalance, this unconsciously ordained tunnel vision of life, which the Mystique fosters. It will, in all likelihood, be only partially
modified when the American Dream reestablishes its roots
in reality.

The Heroic Imperative

In the preface to *The Lady's Not For Burning*, Christopher
Fry quoted a convict who falsely confessed to a murder in
February 1947: "In the past I wanted to be hung. It was
worthwhile being hung to be a hero, seeing that life was

not really worth living." The Mystique, in the form of the Heroic Imperative, has a habit of leading men to their demise.

While the original Greek heroes are regarded as famous dead individuals who came to be worshiped as quasi-divine, they may have been real or imaginary ancestors or "faded gods," ancient deities who for some reason were demoted to human status. While the Homeric hero was a noble and a fighting human, some, like Hector, Achilles, and possibly Hercules, later became objects of worship. Our contemporary heroes may be somewhat less than godlike, but the Mystique has enshrined the heroic as worthy of veneration within the male psyche.

The hero transcends the usual human limitations. He is a representative to men of their archetypal selves, one who epitomizes their grandiose fantasmal images. He is an object upon whom they project their triumphal aspirations, their glorified selves. And woe be to the hero who lets them down! The matador is a case in point. In deliberately defying death in the bullring, he actively embodies the heroic proclivites of the passive spectators in the stands. The "Olés!", the ears and tails awarded for the magnificent performance, are votive offerings accorded not only to the matador, but to the heroic ideal inherent in the primordial egos of his worshipers as well. Should he show timidity, should his spirit flag, he becomes the object of merciless derision and abuse, and must be crucified for it.

Unlike Superman, the hero must be vulnerable. In danger of defeat, dishonor, or death, he must personally confront a presumptively superior adversary and best him in some form of combat. President Clinton's self-glorification as "the comeback kid" neatly nestled into this niche. Despite any duplicity, malevolence, or despicable behavior on the part of his adversary, our paladin must always "play fair" against the odds, and behave in a chivalrous manner. Playing by the Marquis of Queensberry rules, the hero will voluntarily disarm himself if his foe loses his saber or pistol, and continue the battle hand-to-hand. He will never knee his enemy's groin or gouge his eyes. Of course, this code shifts the advantage to the foe, who never indulges in such niceties, but so much the better. While the hero may enjoy the beneficent blessings of divine powers, or have access to supernatural sources, he must never triumph solely because of them.

The hero is seldom motivated by personal material gain. Preferably, he is a fighter against evil and injustice in some form, like saving society or civilization. If he rescues a damsel in distress, it must never be for the eventual insertion of his penis within the warm confines of her pulsating vagina, but rather for the defeat of the damnable forces that imperil her. Otherwise, he is just another Sexual Athlete on the make. Should he fight for the return of the ranch for the tax-sheltered millions it produces each year, he becomes merely an acquisitive capitalist. If the battle is joined because the usurper is an exploitative rotter, the hero's subsequent windfall is incidental, and his heroic credentials remain untarnished.

Like the matador, his feet firmly planted in the sand while facing the devastation of the onrushing bull, the hero is fearless. He faces death with equanimity. With his competence and self-sufficiency assumed, stoicism is the order of the day. A display of "feelings" or "softness" is uncharacteristic for him, since the Heroic Imperative dictates the suspension of emotion, which again raises the hero beyond human expectations. Action displaces caring for. The stereotypical hero generally speaks in monosyllables: "yep" or "nope." Discourse is diversionary and too intellectual, action is all that counts.

Few men are heroes, either to their valets or their families and neighbors. Consequently, the hero is usually a wanderer, one who intrudes into a situation. His background and birth are generally enshrouded in mystery, and his future is symbolized by his riding off toward the sun, whether rising or setting. Where does he go next, presumably to perform other heroic feats? He must ever keep up his employment as a hero; it's part of the contract. This makes it rather rough on the man who opts for the settled family existence, or who attempts to constructively consolidate the social gains of his noble activities.

Above all, the hero is never a coward. The "man's man" never shrinks or cowers. In *Man and Superman*, George Bernard Shaw has Don Juan, the Shavian version of Superman, observe: "He loves to think of himself as bold and bad. He is neither one nor the other, he is only a coward. Call him tyrant, murderer, pirate, bully; and he will adore you, and swagger about with the consciousness of having the blood of the old sea kings in his veins. Call him liar and thief; and he will only take action against you for libel. But call him coward; and he will go mad with rage; he will face death to outface that stinging truth. Man gives every reason for his conduct save one; and that is his cowardice. Yet all his civilization is founded on his cowardice, on his abject tameness, which he calls his respectability."

An illustrative case in point, one which, although it occurred after the Second World War, made an indelible impression on me. Mr. X was hospitalized for medical and psychiatric workup for recurrent "blackouts" and other seemingly self-destructive symptoms of many years' duration. His medical and neurological workups were unremarkable, while the usual psychiatric examination could shed no light on the etiology of his condition. As a desperate measure, a sodium pentothal (truth serum) interview was conducted at considerable depth, which revealed this dimly repressed memory. During the war, Mr. X had not only been a courageous soldier, he had habitually been the leader of his company in barroom brawls and other similar excursions, priding himself on his manhood. During an invasion of a beach in the Pacific, he determined to kill a universally hated lieutenant, a not-so-rare occurrence during wartime. When they hit the beach behind the officer, he called to the lieutenant, who turned back toward him. Mr. X then threw sand in the officer's eyes and shot him. He subsequently repressed the experience as best he could. When this was uncovered during the interview and subsequently discussed in many sessions, the key to the "repression" was not the shooting, which he had always recalled, but the throwing of the sand, which he considered a cowardly act, an act that so conflicted with his manly self-perception that he conveniently "forgot" it, only to pay for it in later years with the aforementioned symptoms. When he finally came to terms with the memory and its implications for his psyche, his symptoms gradually abated. Shaw was right on.

The Mystique has planted the Heroic Imperative deep

within the male breast. Men have leapt into impossible situations, endangering life and limb, in vainglorious attempts
to follow its dictates. In combat, in absurd street situations,
in their pretenses to their children and sweethearts, men
have divested themselves of their rational perspectives in
attempts to assay the tests that the Mystique creates. When
faced with guns, knives, superior numbers, or simply their
inadequacy in the face of the improbable, men should strive
for self-preservation, not heroics. But, as always, the Mystique flays those who do not follow its imperatives, and
men do die rather than face the loss of "masculine self-
esteem."

The Paradise of the Playboy

The essence of the Playboy lies in his very name. He is neither "Playman," nor "Playmaster." Even more pointedly,
one could not even characterize him as a "player," which insinuates the idea of knowledgeability and shrewdness. No,
he is "Playboy"—the puerile prototype, the ever-young-
never-responsible child at play. The eternally youthful
prince, with a world of frolicsome females, fun, and games as
his domain, the Mystique-infused ideal of every red-blooded
American boy. This is "where it's at," what life is, or at least
should be. If this seems a bit exaggerated, think back to the
last half-dozen sitcoms seen on evening TV. Ridiculous
though they may be, this is an image insistently presented to
men, young and old, day after day, night after night.

The Playboy is the fantasied ideal of each man's childhood, now grown taller and operating in an adult world. He is devastatingly attractive to scores of women, who pantingly wait in line to enroll in his harem. These "play-mates," who have apparently cornered the market in massive mammae, are eager and inviting. The Playboy's sexual proclivities and capacities can be equated with those of a rabbit. Hippety-hop, hippety-hop, he leaps and bounds from encounter to encounter. Like the lilies of the fields, he apparently toils not, but oh, how he spins.

His pad is plush and furnished with a plethora of gadgets: stereos, mood lighting, cameras, and poster art. A carefully stocked bar and wine rack fill his playroom, while motorcycles, dirt bikes, and sports cars occupy his garage. His life is filled with leisure time, and any struggle for survival is far beyond his ken. Truly, he is the envy of all red-blooded men.

The male retains his charter membership as a Playboy as long as he keeps his youthful armor and can afford the expense. Where is there to be found an aging, impoverished Playboy? His membership is revoked with age, unless he has accumulated great wealth. In that happy circumstance, he becomes a man of mystery, a "sport," a gay "boule-vardier," or a randy old rascal whose company is courted by the beautiful people. Should his fortunes fail, he becomes a lascivious old lecher and a hanger-on.

The Playboy, as exemplified by the magazine of the same name and others of its genre, happily never has to perform. The "playmates," exposing a cascade of pubic hair or a nipple here and there, provide titillation for happy Playboy fantasies. The male reader becomes a voyeur, under no compulsion to demonstrate feats of sexual derring-do. The editorship is seemingly aware of this, and at times tweaks the proverbial noses of its subscribers. A typical cartoon showed a busty damsel and a moustached Playboy in bed. Our heroine speaks: "Well, if that's what you call sowing your wild oats, you've had a crop failure." It's a funny cartoon. The reader knows that "[t]here but for the Grace of God . . ."

Since the Playboy symbolizes rampant heterosexuality, the homosexual does not fare too well in this milieu. For example, "Playboy's Unabashed Dictionary" defined a "closet queen" as a "male fraud," and a transvestite as a "drag addict," displaying a type of intolerance more appropriate to twelve-year-olds.

The delusion fostered by the Mystique is that the Playboy Paradise is not far from the norm, rather than a seldom-ever land. There are surely some blessed few who have attained this state of perpetual bliss, but there are many more who dwell in its environs, who find their lives more vacuous than exciting. Most large metropolitan areas have their groups of single playboys in their late thirties, forties, and fifties. Those I have known or treated were more often a rather unhappy lot, unable to relate to women over twenty-one years of age, bored with their swinging existence, and incapable of establishing anything resembling a gut relationship with a female peer. Yet the Mystique creates the image, and men are dazzled by it. Not achieving this Sinatra-like state, despite their other successes, many feel they have missed the boat, a lost youth perhaps, a magical carefree state. Perhaps life offers more diverse pleasures than the fictional paradise of the Playboy. The Mystique makes too many men overlook them.

The Dominance Drive

The Dominance Drive is one more illustration of the Mystique's perversion of the normal into the grotesque. Given the hierarchical organization displayed within the many branches of the animal kingdom (i.e., the well-known pecking order) and the evident though currently unmentionable inequalities among members of the human race, some rank order in the societal structure is unavoidable, and must therefore be considered "natural" to some degree. If this be politically incorrect, so be it: it's true nonetheless. While this order is not intrinsically predicated on race, religion, sex, or national origin, apparent inequities in adaptability and capability are undeniable, and consequently eventuate in unequal distribution of power and mastery potential. Less deeply rooted than the biological drives of hunger, thirst, and sex, the human drive toward mastery is nevertheless compelling, and the Mystique has coerced the male into its exaggerated thralldom.

The mastery mode has its genesis in early infancy. Lost and helpless in his initially chaotic universe, the child learns techniques to order and to control it by trial and error. Crying summons aid, subjugation of the anal and urethral sphincter muscles contributes to his sense of autonomy, while the development of locomotor abilities enables him to explore, to become familiar with, and to establish some influence over his environment. The child playing peekaboo with his mother is indulging in a mastership exercise. By volitionally covering his eyes, opening them, and then repeating the process, he symbolically controls his mother's appearance and her disappearance, thus reducing the anxiety occasioned by her departures. As the child matures, the suzerainty stimulus provides him with greater and greater authority over his surroundings, promoting self-assuredness and feelings of competency, a reduction in anxiety, and a propulsion toward further exploration and development of his potentials. In some respects, the mastery motif resembles Ardrey's "territorial imperative." Holding sway over a situation, a circumstance, or a group establishes a niche of one's own, a bastion of security which one can fall back upon, an inviolate territory. What rational and loving parent would deny his or her offspring its emancipation through mastery?

But the Mystique is not a benignant parent. Instead of fostering the healthy modicum of mastery necessary for a comfortable existence, it attempts to saddle men with a drive for dominance, an obsession with power. In its more extreme forms, the Dominance Drive is unlimited in scope and is seldom satisfied.

Who could argue that, leaving aside ethnic, religious, and national considerations for the moment, the Dominance Drive to power by a relatively few individual dictators has resulted in untold millions of deaths just in the last century alone? Were Hitler, Stalin, Mao, and Milosevic merely passive agents of the natural forces of history, or had their Dominance Drives skyrocketed beyond any reasonable control, with humankind paying the price for their pathology? One might liken them to malignant cells, racing around a body's bloodstream, seeking a receptive locus to settle in, fester, and finally destroy the body.

On a more individual basis, Dominance ploys or power plays abound in all areas of the affected man's life—sex, vocation, marriage, recreation, finances. Contaminated by the drive, original purposes and rewards fade, and are replaced by one all-consuming aim, the acquisition of power.

A young man entered psychotherapy complaining of the emptiness and aloneness that pervaded his life. It was soon apparent that his consummate desire to become a millionaire as rapidly as possible had subordinated his interpersonal relationships to a negligible role. Would he really be satisfied with a million or two?

"To be honest, no."

"Five?"

"No."

"Ten million?"

"I know this must sound ridiculous, but I'd go for more."

"What if you owned the entire island of Manhattan?"

"This sounds even crazier, but I'd have to keep going."

His father was a tyrant whose scepter of authority was his checkbook. He talked only of money and punished his wife and children by its withdrawal, exercising power by its use and abuse. His son's recurring fantasy was of stuffing the largest wad of bills attainable down his father's throat. Who could blame him?

Marriages are ruined by monetary power plays. Some husbands attempt to dominate their spouse by doling out the dollars as one would to a child, by making her ask, by giving a daily allowance, or by graciously donating or denying as whim dictates. The attendant humiliation and debasement felt by the wife is as distressing as the poor sex life which generally accompanies it. The infantilization that these husbands are wont to inflict on their dependent spouses adds imaginary inches to their penises. A pity, for their victory proves to be a Pyrrhic one; they make their point but lose the guts of a relationship. A mother-child game consists of the mother clapping the child's hands together while she intones: "Clap hands, clap hands, till Daddy comes home. Daddy has money and Mommy has none." With each repetition of the chant, the child is instilled with the power of the buck, and the dominance of the male who controls it. The Mystique's Dominance Drive gains another adherent.

The delights of sexual coupling are often contaminated by unfortunate dominance ploys. One spouse, husband or wife, by giving or withholding sex from the partner, displays his or her power over the partner. The "missionary position," male atop and female beneath, loses its utilitarian sexual function and becomes a dominance symbol. Some men are threatened to the point of impotency should their mates assume the "superior" position during sexual intercourse, despite the uncomplicated physical fact that the majority of women have their clitoris so situated that it is more easily stimulated in this position, which, in turn, would make their mates feel like superior lovers. "Making it with her," "putting the blocks to her," and "laying her" have their obvious power inferences. Men who take delight in having fellatio performed on them quake at a reciprocal cunnilingus as too unmanly. All too often, sexual stimuli are barely perceived, and are submerged instead in a slew of power fantasies in which the Mystique mutters: "Look how strong and dominant you are," or "You have the power to subdue or hurt, you devil you. Maybe a touch of sadomasochism wouldn't hurt."

Dominance displays are so rampant in the business world that it would require a Machiavelli to write an appropriate compendium. The key to the executive washroom adds little to a man's urinary comfort, but adds much to his hierarchical ranking; a corner office does not materially broaden one's view of the world or enhance one's performance, but it does widen its possessor's range of power. I have listened to top executives of Fortune 500 companies discuss the activities of themselves and their fellow boardroom members. These are men who occupy seats at the pinnacle of economic power, whose golden parachutes literally glisten. Yet they still are frequently compelled to engage in Byzantine conspiratorial plotting to eliminate a rival and gain an additional dollop of power.

Under the aegis of the Dominance Drive, the camaraderie of one's fellows becomes transformed into a viciously aggressive tug-of-war, and man's relationship with women becomes distorted and dehumanized. But the Mystique has absorbed a Nietzschean will to power, and too few men resist it.

The Myth of Male Superiority

The Mystique, like any superb salesman, mixes its pitches. The Achiever Complex and the Dominance Drive are sold softly. But in its propagation of the Myth of Male Superiority, the sell is hard, strident, and simple. The human race is divided into two groups, male and female. The former is innately superior, and is anatomically designed to rule over the latter. Given this divine ukase, the male is to continually exhibit his preeminancy and to live up to his role, day after day, and in any and all situations.

The Myth of Male Superiority is a delusional snare, initially predicated on the possession of a few protruding inches of spongy erectile tissue and a somewhat larger physique. The former, as will be discussed in a subsequent chapter, has been ceremoniously sanctified in almost all cultural institutions, with the possible exception of the obstetrical ward. It reaches ludicrous extremes in the megalomania of machismo and in the assumption of the universality of penis envy in women.

"Macho," a derivative of the Mexican word for "male," has become synonymous with the grandeur of things masculine, in status, pretension, size, and power. The male displaying machismo becomes a strutting peacock, albeit devoid of the latter's delicacy and finery. The swaggering gait, the gross braggadocio, and the readiness to "fight unto death" present a childlike caricature of penile supremacy. Acting under the tyranny of the testicles, the macho fancies himself a warrior, often armed with knife or gun. Should any insult, "dis," or innuendo be directed toward him, he is ready to respond with these penile equivalents. He boasts; he challenges; he preens; he displays. These minor pomposities might be laughable were they confined to only display behavior, but machismo has become a way of life, not only in Mexico and other south-of-the-border regions, but also among many street gangs in the United States. Street fighting allows for the display of one's "balls," and a chance to add oak-leaf clusters to machismal medallions. Shootings and stabbings thus acquire the aura of normalcy in this jungle of the grotesque. And how deeply has this lunacy inserted itelf into international relationships without the powers-that-be having sufficient realization of the aberrancy of it all!

The depreciation of the female is embedded in the machismic core. Women are deemed inferiors, conquests to be made, laid, and boasted of, except, of course, for one's mother, who is placed on an asexual pedestal. The family constellation often found in the machismo culture is characterized by a relatively detached or absent father and a warm mother-son relationship. A strong emotional dependency upon the mother develops as a consequence. The macho male will fight to the death should her honor be impugned, and he displaces his forbidden sexual feelings for her onto other women.

Machomania, rather than representing superiority in the male, portrays man at his worst, as little more than a puppet, controlled by that master puppeteer, the Mystique.

Sigmund Freud stands as one of the premier authentic geniuses of the past century. His solitary voyage into the then uncharted depths of the mind, and the prodigiousness of his discoveries there, have earned him a permanent place in humankind's Hall of Fame. But being human, Freud was not infallible. As a clinician, he was impressed with the material presented by his patients. The women who sought his aid were nurtured in an oppressive Victorian atmosphere, and were largely suffering from hysteria and pseudohysterical illnesses that might be considered schizophrenic today. A deeply rooted envy of the male and his penis was a typical finding in these women of the 1890s and early 1900s. Since Freud was firmly oriented in a biological tradition, he perceived "penis envy" as an inevitable consequence of the genital differences between the sexes, and gave insufficient weight to the cultural factors that may have made their contribution. He went on to conclude that "Anatomy is destiny," with all women fated to hopelessly strive for a penis of their own. The Mystique, never turning down a succulent plum, has heralded this dictum as a scientific verification for its grandiose pretensions. Never mind Freud's other writings on men's anxieties, fear of passivity, dread of castration, and unease when confronted with a vagina! But more about the penis in subsequent chapters.

The concept of male "superiority" is not only questionable, but probably logically untenable. The Mystique, however, is more concerned with impression than with truth. But then, the same can be said of political campaigns, many social conventions, and so many other absurdities by which we live.

By this time it should be obvious that the Reality Inducer will reveal a vast network of syndromes woven by the Mystique to glorify the masculine at the expense of the individual male. The idolatry of Independence, for example, precludes a man's partaking in the mutuality of assistance that a stable society provides and that is essential for a satisfactory life. The man who is unduly independent will "go it alone," never asking directions if he is lost, and can generally be seen at the periphery of any group, opening up to no one, and existing in a not-so-splendid isolation. The portentous patriarch will project a prophetic and fearsome image, the Moses of Michelangelo, replete with a ponderous authority and a paucity of humanity—and on and on it goes.

Since the Reality Inducer is not for sale, I would recommend the following. Periodically pretend that you are a visiting alien and read the local newspaper with the presumed dispassionate detachment of a foreign anthroplogist. It provides an unparalleled sense of perspective. On any page one finds the cultural assumptions, the loaded clichés and phraseology, all highlighting the distortions and biases of which we are usually unaware. For an additional morsel, closely examine the advertisements. With what subtle distortions are you being seduced, how are they trying to take you? As the alien observer, what would you tell the folks back home? What are we like? What are our tribal customs, collective beliefs, illusions and delusions? The basic idea is to put distance between your assumptions and your reality. Detachment invites perspective; and perspective is conducive to a more realistic appraisal of what's really going on in your life.

Although the Masculine Mystique deals with distortions of reality, it must eventually come face-to-face with the facts of men's lives. Let's see how it fares.

2

The Male in the Masculinity Maze

His life was gentle, and the elements
So mix'd in him that Nature might stand up
And say to all the world, "This was a man!"
—WILLIAM SHAKESPEARE

Once upon a time, I spent thirteen windswept hours on a fourteenth-floor ledge with a young man who seemed determined to jump. In addition to his despondency, he was suffering from a duodenal ulcer that had him doubled over in spasmodic pain. After some three to four hours, I felt reasonably certain that he would no longer voluntarily jump, but two problems presented. First, his abdominal pains unsteadied him on our four-foot-wide ledge, which was being buffeted by what seemed like a gale. Additionally, he could not bring himself to reenter the window without seeming a "wimp" and losing his masculine image. Bizarrely, his eventual, albeit unstated, solution, was to continue our dialogue for an additional nine agonizing hours, and then to allow for a media-covered "heroic rescue" to bring him in, thus saving both his manhood and his life. Obviously, it worked for him, but he had come within inches of ending up a bloody splattered mess on the concrete two hundred feet below.

But countless other men have been less fortunate, and have needlessly died trying to live up to some phantasmal masculine ideal; children playing "chicken," young men befuddled in battle, aging men straining in the arms of their nubile mistresses. Others have shackled themselves to demanding careers or abnegated their humanity in a relentless drive for power in attempts to validate their virility. What are they demonstrating? What are they proving? In the quest for "manhood," what is the Holy Grail? Surely, there is more to masculinity than muscles and genitals. In our quantified society, what is the measure of a man?

A satisfying definition of "maleness" or "masculinity" has yet to be delineated. *Webster's New World Dictionary of the American Language* defines "male" as "designating or of the sex that fertilizes the ovum of the female and begets offspring: opposed to female," as if his reproductive function were his sole distinguishing hallmark. "Masculine" connotes: "(1) male, of men or boys; (2) having qualities regarded as characteristic of men and boys, as strength, vigor, boldness, etc., manly, virile; (3) suitable to or characteristic of a man," emphasizing the muscular. Feminine qualities are defined as "gentleness, weakness, delicacy, modesty, etc.; womanly." Questions arise. Is an infertile male lacking in maleness? Is the homosexual or the misogynous man deficient in his masculinity? Are gentleness and modesty unmanly? Are all intellectual snobs effete? And just to stretch it a bit, is the alpha male who sends a missile to blow up a factory in the Sudan more manly than the couch potato who watches behemoth warriors knock each other's brains out in a football stadium on TV? Is a Donald Trump, blatantly broadcasting a glitzy virility and sexual triumph, more of a mensch than a concerned but modest mentor to the next generation? Obviously one can go on and on in this vein, with chaos being added to confusion. I would suggest that maleness or masculinity, the societal manifestation and appreciation of maleness, is a phenomenon composed of three elements: biological, psychological, and social, and so its definition is, like Gaul, divided into three parts.

The biological encompasses the possession of the requisite sexual organs found in the male, the penis, the testicles, and accessory plumbing apparatus such as the seminal vesicles and prostate gland. Add the secondary sexual characteristics, the typical male hair distribution, a lower-pitched voice than the female, a skeletal structure with a more narrow and shallower pelvis, heavier bone structure, and so on, with appropriate allowances made for the age of the man. The more subliminal factors, such as odor and gait, are more subtle undertones. All the above were created and supported by a subterranean stream of testosterone coursing through all the vascular channels of the body. Albeit invisible to the naked eye, it is the fountain that provides the nourishment for that which is masculine.

The psychological includes a man's sense of himself as a member of the male sex, identifying with other men of other places and other times. It incorporates a natural acceptance of his manhood, coupled with the capacity to project this feeling about himself to other people. Add some positive relatedness to the female sex, real or imagined.

The societal involves being perceived as distinctly male by other members of one's society, both male and female. The man's partaking, to some reasonable extent, in the varied activities and roles normative for the male in his particular society would be incorporated. This societal aspect is flexible in a changeable social milieu. It can be generally assessed, however, at a particular point in time. For example, physical strength and muscular prowess may have been a more essential component of masculinity in the nineteenth century than it is in the third millennium.

Utilizing this tripartite conceptual framework, let's add some body to the skeleton.

The Biological Basis of Masculinity

The fundamental similarities and differences between men and women are represented in the chromosomal structure of every cell in the body. Of the forty-six chromosomes in each cellular nucleus, the twenty-two pairs of autosomes, the body chromosomes, are alike in both sexes. When the Frenchman shouts "Vive la différence!" he is referring to only one of the two sexual chromosomes in each nucleus. A woman possesses two X chromosomes, while the man has one X and one Y chromosome. The Y chromosome is the hallmark and starting point of maleness, for it programs the anatomy and the endocrine system of the male embryo.

The primary function of the Y chromosome appears to be the inducement of the primitive embryonal gonads to develop into testes rather than ovaries. Its absence will result in the development of ovaries, with femaleness the consequence. Once the testes develop, during the sixth to twelfth week of intrauterine life, the Y's initiatory role is finished, and the developing gonad now takes over this delicate developmental mosaic. Tiny testicles begin to produce minuscule doses of androgens, the male sex hormones. "Hormone" is derived from the Greek *hormon*, meaning "to stimulate or excite." They are chemical substances produced in various glands and organs of the body, which, when released into the bloodstream, exert their stimulatory or occasionally inhibitory effects on distant "target organs" elsewhere in the body. Thus the thyroid-stimulating hormone produced by the pituitary gland stimulates the thyroid gland to produce its hormones and regulates the body metabolism. In like fashion, the primitive testicle produces its androgens, primarily testosterone, that "masculinize" the fetus. Under the influence of testosterone and an associated hormone that inhibits development of the female reproductive apparatus, a penis rather than a clitoris develops from the primordial genital tubercle, and a scrotum develops in lieu of the vaginal lips. Beyond these evident and elemental anatomical results, testosterone floods the developing brain, and specifically "masculinizes" it, hardwiring it, in a sense, to better handle mathematics and tasks that require spatial conceptualization. Investigation into the proclivity differentials between the brains of both sexes is in its infancy, and offers exciting possibilities in the future. At the base of the brain, just above the pea-sized pituitary gland, lies a critical constellation of neurons known as the hypothalamus. Only .3 percent of the total brain weight, it is involved in such crucial bodily processes as temperature regulation, rage and hunger responses, sexual behavior, and other essentials. Instead of the cyclical production of the two female sex hormones, estrogen and progesterone, the masculinized hypothalamus is involved, via the pituitary, in the steady stimulation of the testicle to produce a constant testosterone stream in the male, and controls the characteristic male behavior during sexual activity. Adjacent neuronal areas mediate erections, aggressivity, oral activities, and smell, all of which are involved in sexual responses. In all likelihood, excitation of the cells in one area spills over to their neighbors, eventuating in variations of sexual activities within the erotic stew.

While testosterone is the hormone of maleness, the two primary sex hormones in women are estrogen and progesterone, both manufactured by the ovaries. Estrogen induces the enlargement of the breasts, the functional responsivity of the vagina, the characteristic hair and subcutaneous fat distribution, et cetera. In brief, estrogen is involved with those external features that label an individual a female. Progesterone, manufactured by the ovary after each monthly ovulation, prepares the various organs to receive and nurture a fertilized egg and to support an ensuing pregnancy. It stimulates the milk-secreting glands in the breast to enlarge and perform, resulting in the breast engorgement many women feel prior to their periods, and effectuates changes in the lining of the uterus to enable the fertilized egg to firmly implant in the uterine wall. Estrogen is the dominant hormone of the first half of the menstrual cycle, while progesterone becomes increasingly dominant in the second half, after ovulation has occurred. The increased sexual interest most women feel during the middle of their cycle is probably a manifestation of hormonal fluctuation, while the male, with his steady hormonal flow, is more constant in the levels of his sexual interest. Parenthetically, most men have somewhat higher testosterone levels in the morning, when the cock crows, so to speak. Wives and lovers might be advised to incorporate such tidbits.

Testosterone appears to be the major hormonal factor influencing the strength of the sexual drive, even in women. Lying atop each kidney are the adrenal glands, which manufacture adrenaline and a host of steroid hormones. Among these are small amounts of testosterone and estrogen in both men and women. Women who have had their adrenal glands surgically removed experience a marked reduction in their sexual drive and clitoral sensitivity. Women who have received testosterone injections frequently experience a dramatic upsurge in their sexual interest and drives. It appears to increase the blood supply to, and the sensitivity of, the clitoris. Ergo, testosterone is one of the few known aphrodisiacs. But alas, what nature giveth, nature taketh away, since excess amounts of androgens masculinize a woman, unfortunately negating the utility of testosterone in this area. Testosterone seems to lend immediacy and activity to the sexual drive, which may account for the "Wham, bam, thank you, mam" component of the male's sexual activity, while the woman, less influenced by it, is more leisurely paced sexually, and is longer lasting in her erotic activities. My experience with men given testosterone to enhance their potency has been that it only rarely has increased their erectile size, but it usually gives them a swagger, a feeling of aggressiveness and increased confidence. What would happen if we added it to the water supply?

Despite the assertions of some feminist writers that psychosexual personality is primarily a postnatal and learned phenomenon, there is a rapidly developing body of knowledge to the contrary, indicative of psychosexual predisposition existing either in utero, or at least prior to the introduction of any form of social conditioning. Girl babies differ from boy babies, not only by virtue of their vaginas, but by inborn psychological proclivities as well.

Aggressivity, a presumptive male characteristic, is thought to be primarily the result of environmental conditioning (i.e., give the kid a toy gun and have him go bang-bang). But even infant male chimpanzees are more aggressive and more initiatory in their play than their sisters, who appear more adept with their hands and try to communicate more with each other. Standing across a room, one should be able to distinguish a cage of infant female chimps from a cage of infant male chimps solely by their play behavior. Furthermore, if a female monkey, pregnant with a female fetus, is injected with testosterone at a particular stage in the gestation period, a biologically female infant will emerge, but one who engages in the rough-and-tumble play characteristic of the male. While it is admittedly questionable to extrapolate directly from primate to human, it would be even more foolhardy to evade the probable inferences. If one carefully observes the behavior of human infants, let's say below the age of three, it is difficult not to be reminded of early primate behavior. This is not to say that sexual role and behavior is only a chemical derivative. But there are distinctive psychosexual differences between male and female that simply cannot be dismissed as merely societal indoctrination, although the precise chemistries and neuroanatomical connections have yet to be delineated. The expression of these differences is involved in the biological aspect of maleness and masculinity. The biological maturation of the fetus is followed by, and interlaced with, the psychological adaptation of the child to his gender.

The Psychological Factor

A sine qua non of masculinity involves a man's sense of himself as the male of the species, with a positive reaction to the fact of his maleness. He "knows" that he is the male in his society, and rather likes the idea.

The "core gender identity," a firmly fixed conviction that "I am a male" or "I am a female," is ineradicably set before the third year of life. In all likelihood, it is the consequence of some form of human imprinting, the fixation of a behavior pattern during an early formative period, due to genes, chemistry, or God knows what.

Once the core gender identity has taken root, the young boy moves off to develop his "core gender role," which can be described as those things that a person says and does to disclose himself or herself as having the status of a boy or man, girl or woman, respectively. It includes, but is not restricted to, sexuality in the form of eroticism. Gender role is appraised in relation to the following: general manner-

isms, deportment, and demeanor; play preferences and recreational interests; spontaneous topics of talk in un-
prompted conversation and casual comment; content of
dreams, daydreaming, and fantasies; replies to oblique in-
quiries and projective tests; evidence of erotic practice and
finally, the person's own replies to direct inquiry. I would
also add an entity akin to "streetsmart," namely "malesmart," which refers to some more ephemeral subliminal
manifestations of maleness. For example, the male exhibits
his own unique behavior at a crap, blackjack, or poker table. This is much less evident, and often not the case at
the bridge table, especially when women are playing. He
handles the payment of restaurant checks differently. Men
are more prone to reflexively split the check, while women
often separately add their tabs. Men occupy space more
broadly as they saunter down the street, are less apt to
bargain in stores, and shun asking directions or soliciting
help. Linguistically, the appreciation and use of four-letter
words is an obvious male attribute, although there are
women who do try. Displays of mutual affection between
males are there, but are far more implicit and implied than
those of their female brethren. Briefly then, what is being
dealt with here is a male "feel," in contrast to the female.

Inherent in a positive acceptance of one's maleness, a
feeling of comfort with one's genitals is included. It is not
uncommon to find a man unable to urinate in a public
men's room due either to feelings of inadequacy about his
penis, or a fear that he will betray his masturbatory history
or proclivities. Many men feel their penis to be "too small."
In actuality, significant differences in size of the erect penis

are rare and inconsequential. Regardless of the dimensions of the flaccid (nonerect) phallus, most erect penises stand equally tall for all practical purposes. Similarly, there is no relation between a man's physique, large or short, and his penile size. A man comfortable with his maleness is unconcerned with genital gigantism. In a similar vein, the woman's "cunt hatred" of which Germaine Greer writes, is symptomatic of an impairment in a woman's femininity. An aversion to any normal part of one's anatomy is pathologic, until proven otherwise. Ensconced in his maleness, a man instinctively develops a capacity to project what Saul Bellow referred to as a "message of gender," akin to the previously mentioned "malesmart." One need not be a muscle-bound Mr. America or a cigarette-smoking cancer-prone cowboy to impress the populace with one's maleness. Just as a natural athlete impresses us with his competence by his ease of gesture, a maximum of accomplishment with a minimum of effort, the comfortable male radiates the totality that one associates with the male gender.

As the boy sprouts, he develops a concept of himself vis-à-vis the opposite sex. In our culture, his primary lessons are learned from his give-and-take with his mother or mother surrogates. During these interactions, he incorporates a lifelong impression of how women feel toward him and vice versa. An affectionate and interested mother bequeaths to her son a positive expectation from other women, a feeling of being important and worthwhile. By acting in accordance with this expectation as he develops, he is likely to obtain precisely this response from the future women in his life. During this interplay, his father hopefully will serve as an approving, nonthreatening, solid masculine model who reinforces the child's aspirations both as a male and a human being.

During the period of life between the fourth and the eighth year, dramatically referred to as the Oedipal phase, a boy becomes to some degree "erotically" attached to his mother and simultaneously comes to regard his father as a rival. One often hears the youngster asking such questions as "Dad, if you die, do I get your ties?", or house keys or other similar variation. Should the father be sufficiently doltish, he will regard these as bona fide threats, seriously regarding his son as a rival, and engendering the seeds of a lifelong contentious relationship. If his mother responds positively, and his father doesn't regard it as too personally threatening, the boy is imbued with an assertive component to his sexuality, thus extending and amplifying his gender role. A negative and destructive maternal relationship, on the other hand, will raise doubts and anxieties about the boy's future dealings with women. An overly demanding and rejecting mother can easily induce a sense of inadequacy in her son. The young boy simply is not equipped to deal with a superabundance of maternal sexuality and paternal threat.

I have been impressed with a seeming lack or distortion in their projection of gender in many men who were reared, during their formative years, in homes devoid of involved women. As adults, they are basically indifferent, denigratory, or outwardly hostile to women as human beings, and, despite the fact that some marry, they expect little from women as people, as lovers, as wives, and as mothers of their children.

Misogynists have a flaw in their masculinity. That portion of a male's personality that proclaims: "You are a woman, and an attraction exists between us because I am a man" is not apparent. A healthy young boy, equipped with the biological and psychological necessities of malehood, brings these attributes into play within the cultural area of the masculine mosaic.

The Societal Sector

The social component of masculinity is predicated on a male's adherence to some norms within his society, and a reliance on these norms to indicate the range of roles he may comfortably play. This by no means describes what should be, but concentrates rather on what currently is. I know of no past or present social grouping in which there has been no significant difference between male and female dress, behavior, activities, and status. These aspects are the most fluid, most variable, and most exclusively socially indoctrinated aspects of masculinity. They change with time, culture, and mores, being least static in periods of rapid cultural change, such as we are currently experiencing. While one can discuss generally accepted concepts of masculinity from an historical vantage point, it is probably impossible for anyone to accurately and specifically delineate the male social role at the time in which he lives, especially if conditions are in a state of flux. The best an observer can hope for is to impart a general assessment of the male's role in a reasonably objective fashion.

Perhaps the most historically representative, and certainly among the earliest, philosophical prototypes of masculinity and femininity were devised and written down in the *I Ching* during the mists of pre-Confucian China, some three thousand years ago, with the formulation of the principles of Yang and Yin. The Tao, the rhythm and sense of the universe, encompassed these two elemental forces. Yang, the male principle, had the attributes of activity, positivism, production, light, and life. Yin, the female principle, was passive, negative, earthy rather than spiritual, dark, cold, and dead. The Tao contained both these elements in a constant dynamic equilibrium, with one complementing the other. With but occasional exceptions, the extension of these principles has persisted in varied cultural mystiques to the present day. The active and productive male, the passive female; the enlightened man, the silly woman; the spiritually uplifted male, the priest, Jesus, versus the earthy woman with the darkness of her womb, and so forth, can all be readily viewed within the Yang-Yin framework. How much more deeply ingrained are these atavistic concepts than are the rags and snails and puppy dogs' tails as the formative ingredients of young males, and the sugar and spice and everything nice as the constituents of little girls. Throughout recorded history, the male role has been the aggressor, the active doer of deeds. The woman has been attached to the home and hearth, "Kinde, Küche, Kirche," the consort and simultaneously the opponent of Yang. In this most balanced of philosophical constructs, the balance always seemed to swing toward Yang. One can always counter this by mentioning Queen Elizabeth, the Amazons, or Joan of Arc, but they are the rare exceptions, and Joan was burned for it. The woman's role was still circumscribed, and any deviations were ipso facto excluded from the boundaries of femininity.

However, as Tennyson observed, "The old order changeth, yielding place to new. And God fulfills Himself in many ways." One can only hope that if God is presently fulfilling himself, he has a reasonably good idea of what he is doing. With the maturation of social consciousness in our society, class distinctions are losing their imperatives, and the class "female" is asserting herself, demanding more equitable if not preferential treatment, and getting it. Men find themselves currently at sea, seeking an adequate lodestar to follow, a guiding principle to which they might hitch their masculine identities.

For the foreseeable future, men might be expected to gravitate toward those social roles in which they are more likely to excel, taking into account the exigencies inherent in the most fluid social structure since civilization was invented. While no one is presently in a position to define these areas, we do have some helpful hints.

Erik Erikson's classic experiment is a case in point. One hundred and fifty school-age boys and an equal number of school-age girls were presented with a group of dolls, of both child and adult varieties, animals, furniture, toy automobiles, and blocks. They were then asked to construct "an exciting scene from an imaginary moving picture." The girls' creations were primarily representations of "inner space." They concentrated on the interior of houses, or enclosed their buildings with doll figures situated within the walls. The atmosphere was relatively peaceful, although intrusions by dangerous men and animals were not uncommon. The boys, on the other hand, built high towers, walls with obvious protrusions, and concentrated on external scenes, with moving automobiles and animals. They produced frequent automobile accidents, robberies with the thief being apprehended, collapsing buildings, and ruins. These ruins were found exclusively in the boys' constructions. Whether these creations are representative of the "somatic" or bodily configuration of the individual girl or boy is questionable. They may portray castration anxiety in boys with the expectation of being caught and "ruined," or they may have merely expressed the social conditioning to which these youngsters had already been exposed. These questions are, for the moment, beside the point. This experiment does, at the least, represent interest and attitudinal differences presently within our culture that indicate predilections in social role. Although Erikson's work is a product of the mid-twentieth century, it remains remarkably descriptive of observations being made even today.

The functionalist school of sociology, under the aegis of Talcott Parsons, conceptualized the masculine role as "instrumental," with the associated traits of aggressiveness, tenacity, curiosity, ambition, planning, responsibility, originality, and self-confidence. Parsons characterized the feminine role as essentially "expressive," as evidenced by affection, sympathy, obedience, cheerfulness, kindliness, and friendliness to both adults and children. He also added negativity and jealousy, which sounds suspiciously like the Yin. While he may be somewhat wide of the target, once again the male is seen as the active instrumental agent, while the woman is perceived as the fountain of emotionality, the sentinel of the senses. The fact that one-third of senior American officials are women, including two justices of the Supreme Court and one ex–secretary of state, somewhat belies the dead-on accuracy of this construct, but the "instrumental" and the "expressive" do have a certain resonance.

Other studies reveal no significant differences in intelligence between men and women. Boys may have a greater facility with mathematics and spatial relations, while girls have a greater verbal fluency, and a more rapid rate of intellectual and emotional development up to the start of their college years, when male-female differentials begin to equalize.

While "superiority" in male-female matters is a ludicrous subject to pursue, given some of the differences previously alluded to, these items do indicate areas of greater male suitability and comfort when contrasted with those of women. These aptitude areas exist on a pragmatic basis despite current cries for "sexual equality," political correctness, and the pandering of politicians. A few examples. With the testosterone-induced aggressiveness, rashness, and rapidity of the male, he is better suited to become a day trader in the stock market than his sister, while her maternal orientation might make her a head of state less likely to bomb the opposition. The male is more like to survive in combat, while his sister, possessing less of the necessary physical aptitude, is more apt to diminish the confidence and bonding within the squad, despite calls for equality in combat opportunities. While I would much prefer to be protected by a stronger, more immediacy-oriented fireman or police officer, given the insistence of HMOs on speeded-up patient visits I might prefer my future physician to be female, relying on her nutritive impulses to prolong my visit, if necessary. Why not make a game of this at your next dinner party? See what your guests come up with.

It is commonplace for a psychiatrist to treat men and women who are convinced that they are "latently homosexual." Men may feel that they have failed as "men" by not emerging as champions in our competitive business world where every other man seems to be buying the Taj Mahal with profits from the Internet, or women may be unable to resolve their desire to be sexually expressive with the conviction that a "woman" must be passive to be feminine. Some, unable to grasp a cohesive sense of their own masculinity or femininity in the face of ill-defined or caricatured cultural impressions, deny any differences. And so we ogle at the abnegation of sexual roles. Up with unisex!

Since our subject is Adam, one might construct an admittedly artificial "Masculinity Index," extrapolated from the previous discussion. Its purpose is neither to tag nor to label, but rather to provide the questioning male with something more objective by which he might gauge that most elusive of qualities, his masculinity.

The Masculinity Index

Consider a theoretical spectrum, ranging from a male all but devoid of the aura of masculinity, the omega male, at one end, to the superman at the other. Please note that the spectrum does not range from masculinity to femininity. A male is a male, regardless of his appearance, and he will automatically turn toward the door marked "Gents" rather than "Ladies." The scale is constructed from the three attributes previously elaborated (Biological, Psychological, and Societal), and the personal weighting may vary with a man's age and his life circumstances.

The Biological

1. Possession of the male genital apparatus. Unless the penile size is *measurably* smaller than the average five and a half or six inches when standing tall, worry not, you're okay. Forget limpid measurements; they have no significance.

2. Penile utilization (i.e., premature ejaculation, impotency, perpetual priapism, satyriasis, and the like) is not a measure of masculinity per se, but may rather indicate some physical or psychological problem that is apt to be a treatable problem instead of a stigma. Some presumptively "hypermasculine" film heroes were reportedly said to be lousy lovers by the women who should know, while the supposedly sexless Toulouse-Lautrec sexually sported with the models and entertainers of Montmartre.

3. Possession of the appropriate secondary sexual characteristics of the male. This would include a lower-pitched voice, an angular rather than a curvaceous bodily outline, the male hair distribution. The muscles need not be mammoth, nor the voice deep and sonorous, for we are dealing with the average rather than the unusual.

The Psychological

1. A sense of comfortably belonging to the male sex including:
   a. Core gender identity
   b. Comfort with one's core gender role
   c. A happy acceptance of one's sexual apparatus as normal.
2. The capacity to project the above.
3. A positive acceptance of one's malehood, as evidenced by dreams, daydreams, and fantasies.
4. Identification with other men.
5. Finding women generally attractive.
6. The feeling that one has some attractiveness to women.

The Societal

1. Being viewed by others in the society as securely ensconced in the male segment of the culture.
2. Society's positive reaction to one's projection of gender.
3. A reasonable degree of partaking in the society's gender norms. This would include mannerisms, "malesmarts," deportment, interests, vocational and avocational preferences.
4. Anything that delineates a man as individual or unique, without detracting from him as a person.

   In accentuating a man's distinctive qualities, his other assets are correspondingly highlighted and increasingly appreciated. The stamp of uniqueness has a transcendent appeal (e.g., Elvis Presley).

An additional dimension was supposedly added to the masculine dilemma during the presidential campaign of 2000 when it was revealed that Al Gore had employed the services of a feminist writer, Naomi Wolf, to transform him from a beta to an alpha male. The news sent men scurrying to refresh their Greek, and to fret over pronouncements of ethnologists and primatologists. These students of mammalian behavior had long recognized the existence of hierarchical rankings within all species, in which the possessor of maximal strength and resources put a male on top of the heap, endowing him with the ultimate in power and sexual access. His less effective competitors were consigned to beta and gamma positions, ending in omega. But before one's alphabetical maleness becomes too deeply engraved in the masculine assessment, consider the following: the primary alpha male of our universe, the president of the United States, made himself the object of scorn and late-night TV jokes due to his pathetic mishandling of his sexual peccadilloes, and Al Gore suffered acute embarrassment from his attempts at image-altering that may have cost him the presidency. Simultaneously, the presumptive nerds of the world, the omega males who hide behind their computers, were well on their way to cornering the monetary supply of the world. Ergo, in matters of male hierarchy, suspend judgment.

While the above system is clearly somewhat arbitrary, it serves to delineate "where one stands" in the male spectrum. It should, in fact, be modified to conform to the realities of one's life. Thus the Biological and Psychological should be endowed with greater weight in the preteen and teen years, before the boy has had the opportunity to develop the Societal elements to their fullest. The older, or aging, man should have sufficiently developed the Psychological and the Societal so that his sagging musculature and diminished energy and sexual reserves will be more than compensated for. A man who has undergone castration, or who has dealt with impotency as a consequence of surgery for cancer of the prostate gland, would still feel quite masculine, relying on a well-developed sense of his manhood in the Psychological and Societal spheres. Masculinity is, after all, a totality, and I can think of numerous men, either advanced in years or suffering physical infirmity, who exude it to a greater degree than their younger and healthier counterparts. Additional adjustments for more controversial areas, i.e., homosexuality and transvestitism, must be made, but it would be premature for one to adequately attempt it until the political heat has somewhat abated.

It should be apparent that there is no passing or failing grade in this index. I have never seen a man who was just biologically male, although I have known more than a few thugs, nor have I met a truly composite Everyman. No one in our complex culture can ever develop perfectly, or even evenly, in all areas. A man who relies exclusively on his rugged good looks or muscular physique (the biological) may fail to develop the psychological or societal. The "professional" male, the doctor, lawyer, or Indian chief oftentimes is so dependent on the societal that his biological and psychological areas suffer. The vast majority of men will find enough of themselves in this index. Those who still harbor serious questions about their presumptive inadequacy might be well advised to seek a professional consultation.

3

Man's Wonderful Workaday World

A spectacular astral explosion, one monumental miscalculation, and Earth was born. Chaos, cataclysm, fire, and brimstone reigned until, the elements exhausted, quiet descended. The primordial slime set, and the volcanic ooze slithered back into the bowels of the earth. The vaporous mists, writhing and consolidating, ascended, vaulting the Earth in a panoply of incandescent clouds. The rains washed the land and gave rise to the seas. Mother Nature, now liberated from the prison of an inimical planet, borrowed a pinch of lightning from heaven, added it to a stew of oceanic amino acids, and created life.

First the algae and amoebae, the plankton and the protozoa, then the fishes, reptiles, and dinosaurs; some recipes worked while others were locked away in eternal evolutionary file cabinets, never to be reopened. The final dish, the ultimate in design, dramatically culminated in the creation of Woman, the "first sex," in Mother Nature's own image. In a burst of maternal exuberance, women were endowed with the Earth, with all its proliferating blessings. The fertile plains, the kaleidoscopic foliage, the fruits of the trees, the songs of the birds, all theirs! The primeval primogenitors of the human race, Daughters of Nature, the planet belonged to them!

Ecstatic in their newly inherited domain, women formally celebrated their uniquely acquired state with the organization and first meeting of the Prehistoric Alliance of Women. Though naked, these procreators of humanity were not naïve. The primary item on the agenda was the issue of continuing their survival in the happiest of habitats. Blessed with Mother Nature's foresight, they perceived the evident necessity for the creation of a "Provider," a creature to bear the brunt of the heavy work, the abundance of onerous responsibilities, the monetary concerns, the pressures of time, deadlines, worries, commuting, and the assembling of fix-it-yourself toys.

The more pragmatic of the celebrators anticipated certain difficulties. How were they to keep the Provider in perpetual servitude and yet motivated to perform its assigned tasks? An ad hoc committee was appointed, and after much discussion in the local sylvan watering hole, reported its deliberations. The problem had proven simpler than at first conceived. Grant the Provider a penis to glorify (and to fertilize the female's eggs), a more massive physique and larger muscles to feel stronger and more powerful (and to do the heavy work), and a Masculine Mystique to live by. The proposal for the creation of the Provider was then presented to Mother Nature as a nonnegotiable demand. Her capitulation was a happy one, with amnesty granted to all demonstrators. The Provider was instantly created from a pubic hair, and was henceforth referred to as "less-than-woman," or simply "Man." With the formulation of the Grand Matriarchal Scheme, the meeting was adjourned.

Eons elapsed. The minutes of the first meeting of PAW have descended into the dusts, and with them the aims and purposes of the Grand Scheme. Modern woman, or a segment thereof, alienated from the designs of her forebears, aspires to what she now envisions as male vocational "prerogatives," and the Feminist Movement is undertaken, the dire and unintended consequences of which will be addressed in later chapters.

The Grand Matriarchal Scheme is perhaps whimsical, yet the theme of an actual patriarchal cabal, both explicit and implicit in much of Feminist writing, presents only the other side of this fantastic coin. It betrays either a lack of knowledge, or a gross misunderstanding, of the realities of the individual male's existence, for Man's Wonderful Workaday World is sometimes less than the unremitting pleasure it is reputed to be.

The image of the Provider, a critical component of the Masculine Mystique, has been uncritically accepted by men as a fact of their glorified lives. The Dominance Drive, the Achiever Complex, and the Myth of Male Superiority find the Provider a superb instrument for their expression.

The Mystique has bequeathed the Provider an ethic: the more productive and prolific his endeavors, the more virtuous the man. Hard work, ambition, and diligence are extolled as praiseworthy, since they further the purpose for

which he was created, while idleness, "unproductive" leisure, and a lack of financial wizardry become somewhat
sinful and tainted. Beneath expressions of sorrow for the
man who "worked himself to death" lie feelings of admiration for a fallen hero. That he may have been foolish, and
more neurotic than noble, is seldom stated. He must have
been "a good man." And so one of the greatest dramas of
the past century is *Death of a Salesman*.

The Darwinian era of economic thought has gone beyond the imprint of "the survival of the fittest" to their
deification, with Bill Gates, Steve Case, and Michael Eisner
becoming a new version of the Holy Trinity. In lieu of their
appearing as subjects of illuminations in medieval biblical
manuscripts, their ubiquitous portraits grace the covers of
most magazines. By flaunting such examples, the Mystique
has enshrined performance and success as among the very
noblest of male virtues. How else can one explain the crush-
ing work schedules and the devotion of most of a man's
waking hours to the pursuit of vocational success? "Economic necessity," the usual reply, is an insufficient answer.
Too many men work, or would work if they could, over
and beyond the time required to provide a reasonable standard of living. Furthermore, each step up the ladder makes
necessities out of prior luxuries, and, given the male's sus-
ceptibility to every new advertising pitch that comes across
his plate, higher standards and greater luxuries loom just
beyond the horizon. Must one be the first on his block to
acquire a high-density TV set, the fastest modem known
to mankind, or the flashiest suburban sports vehicle? But
the Provider must keep working and amassing, for, to him,
"life" and "work" are synonyms.

The Bhagavad Gita tells us: "What is work, and what is not work, are questions that perplex the wisest of men." A dictionary definition of work is: "Physical or mental effort exerted to do or make something; purposeful activity, labor, toil." Its essential purpose is to provide the essentials of life for a man and his family. While the fortunate male derives varying degrees of satisfaction from his labor, surveys indicate that 60 to 80 percent of workers are dissatisfied with their vocational lot, and would switch jobs if given the opportunity.

From Saint Benedict's benediction "To work is to pray," to Aldous Huxley's "Like every man of sense and good feeling, I abominate work," work has been alternately lauded and lambasted. Euripides referred to toil as "the sire of fame," while William Faulkner wryly noted: "One of the saddest things is that the only thing a man can do for eight hours a day, day after day, is work. You can't eat for eight hours a day, nor drink for eight hours a day, nor make love for eight hours." Although most men find their labors to be somewhere between these extremes of heaven and hell, it would appear that more are aware of the heat of the Inferno than feel the flutter of angel's wings.

From the standpoint of Saint Benedict, it might be said that a man's occupation gives him a sense of identity, akin to: "Who are you?", "I'm a lawyer." It has a regulatory effect on one's life, allowing achievement and mastery in a specific area, while encouraging the derivation of satisfaction from the exercise of one's talents. Moreover, work affords the obsessional personality a socially applauded outlet for a neurotic compulsion. In our society, the successful worker enhances his self-esteem, a validation of his worth as a human being. There are, unfortunately, too few agencies in our social milieu that lend themselves to this type of validation. A man who is satisfied with his job finds it to be one of his central interests, has some social relationship with his coworkers, and is motivated to seek satisfaction and gratification from his exertions. An interesting and secure job diminishes feelings of insecurity, helplessness, and inferiority. Like it or not, a boy is raised to feel that his self-worth is inextricably bound to his vocation and to his standing on the socioeconomic ladder to extremes. Donald, a thirty-year-old dentist, was summering on Fire Island, a fairly sophisticated spa and retreat for the tired brains of Manhattan. Since his parents were intrigued by the island's reputation, lurid and otherwise, he invited them out for the day. Close friends generously gave a cocktail party in their honor. On a spacious patio, glasses clinked and martinis mixed with gimlets and screwdrivers. Praises of "Donald" were directed toward his wide-eyed parents. During the occasional lull that marks the tempo at such affairs, his mother, her breast swelling with pride, meekly inquired: "Doesn't anyone call him 'Doctor'?" Donald prayed for a quick and merciful death, and proceeded to drown himself in vodka, wishing again and again that he had become a stockbroker. Apparently, occupational status does have its limitations, and the wise man realizes them.

If we approach work from the viewpoint of a Faulkner or a Huxley, we confront alienation, boredom, and psychological slavery. In *The House of the Dead*, Dostoevsky agonized that: "To crush, to annihilate a man utterly, to inflict on him the most horrible of punishments so that the most ferocious murderer would shudder at it and dread it beforehand, one need only give him work, of a completely useless and irrational character." How many men have employment approximating this job description? The factories and the assembly lines, the tollbooths, the manned elevators, the bureaucratic nonwork, and countless other assignments, peopled by unnoticed and unremembered faces, crush the mind, annihilate the spirit, and impose the sentence of a vacuous existence on those employed in them. The consequence of this unhappy state is a sense of alienation, in which a man is divorced from his humanness, feeling more an inanimate "thing" than a human being. While some men consciously "make a deal" with themselves to "put in their time," collect their paychecks, and finally their pensions, other men are aware only of a nagging dissatisfaction or depression, the sense that something isn't quite right with their lives. Alienation, present in varying degrees, is a modern-day version of Limbo, somewhat like a tour of duty on a prison ship, shuttling from Lassitude to Boredom and back.

The "Squeezed" occupy the opposite end of the vocational spectrum. Instead of dying of boredom, they are perishing from being pushed, stretched, and stressed, by themselves or by others, beyond reasonable psychophysiological limits. Air traffic controllers with their stress-induced ulcers, telemarketers, and other workers boxed into small cubicles wearing headsets and staring at computer screens hour after programmed hour, all qualify for citizenship in the Squeeze. So do associates in law firms and hospital interns and residents, with their eighty- to hundred-hour weeks that leave them dazed and distracted, and predisposed toward the commission of errors that impact on their careers and those whose lives and fortunes depend on them. Working more and leisuring less, the personification of the Provider is seen as something spectral.

The psychological enslavement of the Provider to his occupation is more pervasive than is commonly realized, and is strikingly exemplified by the Retirement Depression. There was a time when Stan had been a gregarious and dynamic editor-in-chief of a leading magazine. Having climbed his way from newspaper copy boy to become a leading figure in publishing circles, he had straddled the summit. Under his sixteen-hour-per-day regimen, the publication's circulation had flourished and its quality had appreciated. Totally immersed in his industry, he passingly dealt with the idea of eventual retirement by flip references to "bridge and golf." Inevitably, retirement day arrived, and shockingly so. The testimonials over, he soon found that golf had been interesting only when business was discussed on the back nine, and that bridge could become a deadly bore when played day after day. Time became increasingly oppressive. The precipitating fuse, that final fillip that ushers in a full-blown depression, was the first issue of the publication with Stan's name missing from the masthead. His distraught wife described him as "a changed man overnight." The dynamo had had his plug pulled. He alternately paced, or sat with a drawn, expressionless face. A previously normal blood pressure had soared, and sleep had become a dim memory. His appetite had disappeared, along with any sexual interest, which should not be too surprising since men who have lost their jobs have significant drops in their testosterone levels. "The only thing I can tell you is that my name on the masthead was like a badge, and without it I feel like a powerless eunuch," was his assessment. Heroes who lose their laurel wreaths understandably become depressed.

Stan typifies the man who overly utilizes his job to establish an identity and to keep this identity vital and alive. As part of the contract, however, he becomes enslaved to his position. When the job terminates, his identity evaporates, and he becomes the good plow horse who is lost without his plow. The sympathy and understanding of those about him are of little avail. When a life has lost its meaning, solicitude and concern seem alien. Noël Coward sang: "When you feel your song is orchestrated wrong / why should you prolong your stay?", which about sums it up. The man who stakes his life on his Provider role takes a greater gamble than he realizes, and the piper must eventually be paid.

A gamble of a different sort emerged when I received a consultation request from an orthopedic surgeon to examine a man hospitalized for a paralyzed right arm. The request added: "Please help. He is driving us crazy." The patient's neuromuscular workup was negative, and he seemed curiously unconcerned about his right arm, while having no difficulty in making loud demands of the hospital staff. Since his paralysis was evidently hysterical in origin, his "unconcern" being a classic "la belle indifférence" seen in hysterical illness, I suggested that he be immediately discharged to some outpatient facility, since further hospitalization would only perpetuate the condition. Some months later, I received an emergency page to rush to the doctor's lounge, ASAP, where a circus program was being shown on television. And there, for all to behold, was our ex-patient, swinging from a trapeze! Apparently, acrobatics was the family occupation, from which he felt unable to escape. There had been no malingering here; he had been quite convinced that the paralysis was genuine. The unconscious development of a paralysis enabled him to escape a vocational situation that he felt unable to master otherwise. I wonder, Did we do him a favor . . . ? At any rate, the Provider kept swinging.

The Mystique loudly proclaims the male as the lord and master of his economic domain. The popular myth has him doling out the pesos with a parsimonious palm, with his wife barely making ends meet. But is this verity or merely propaganda? While the Provider labors in the fields "by the sweat of his brow," and ravages the earth for his family's sustenance, it is his wife who dispenses 85 percent of the family income, and seems best equipped to manage the family's assets. A prime complaint voiced by women is that their husbands have no idea of the cost of the various items in the family budget. The complaint is valid, and has been the cause of innumerable family squabbles. Unfortunately, the Provider has become estranged from the utilization of the very money he has earned. On those rare days when a husband accompanies his wife on a shopping tour, the store manager waxes ecstatic. The bill is invariably higher, with the husband happily engaging in impulse buying and in the purchase of the more expensive items, despite the fact that their cost astonishes him. It is as though he is celebrating the expenditure of his earnings, like a vacationer for whom money has lost its meaning.

"Figures don't lie," as that unctuous saying goes, and the numbers on a check become a mathematical calibration of the Provider's prowess, akin to the number of pounds a weight lifter can press. Living in the era of the instant billionaire, today's average Everyman finds himself rather behind the eight ball. His median income in 1997 was $66,393, if he had at least a bachelor's degree, and but $33,611 for the high school graduate. But before we get swept up by the economic tsunami, factor in the 10 percent drop in real earnings since 1970, when inflation is taken into account. In the event that our protagonist pushes to send his son to an Ivy League college, he must come up with $30,000 per year for tuition, room, and board, plus such incidentals as clothing, books, condoms, et cetera. In the good old days, the price of a year in college was equivalent to the cost of a Chevrolet, and the cost of college, in constant dollars, has more than doubled in the last two decades.

To make matters even worse, we are living in an age of rapidly rising expectations, in which accepted and expected standards of living outsoar the capacity of the average wage earner. Surrounded by images of affluence (how many kitchenettes and cramped living rooms are portrayed on television or movie screens?), men feel compelled to procure and display them or suffer a loss of prestige. So welcome moonlighting! In the halcyon days of my internship, ambulance calls sped me to many slum dwellings, dingy and barely furnished, inhabited by undernourished children. It was not a rarity for family members to follow the ambulance back to the hospital in expensive and exquisitely polished automobiles. The appurtenances had taken priority over the appetite.

It has now become generally accepted, by sociologists, economists, et al., that while modern technological advances may have diminished overall work time, the higher earners work longer hours. These "long-houred workers," professionals and executives, are pressured to forgo vacations and to increase the time and effort devoted to work. Blue-collar workers evidence a preference for more paid work rather than leisure time, and keenly compete for overtime. Lightheartedness seems to be on the wane, and it has been my observation that my own colleagues have become increasingly humorously disadvantaged. It should also be noted that men under forty-five who are subject to deadlines, marked competition, and long working hours tend toward higher levels of blood cholesterol and a higher incidence of heart attacks than do their fellows in less stressful vocational milieus, and that this stress may be facilitated by intense ambition itself.

During his sojourn in the occupational jungle, the Provider is beset by numerous pitfalls and snares that entrap his psyche into one disability after the other.

A man's attitude toward his position is determined by his individual personality interwoven with the aspects of the job itself. Security, opportunity for advancement, working conditions, wages, and benefits are immediate and evident considerations. The quality of supervision, the opportunity to participate in the channels of communication with the higher echelons, the intrinsic elements of the job (travel, entertaining, etc.), and the opportunity to identify oneself as part of an organization are less obvious, but are, perhaps, of equal importance. While in Japan, I had the opportunity to visit factories and other places of business. Small Shinto and Buddhist shrines were inconspicuously placed within department store and factory

complexes. "Why are these shrines in commercial loca-
tions?" I asked my interpreter. Somewhat taken aback by
the naïveté of my question, he simply answered: "For the
employees to pray for the success of the company, of
course." They were, in fact, cared for, and this feeling was
reciprocated. The paternalism of Japanese firms, combined
with their liberal bonuses and credit card privileges, increased the worker's identification with his firm, and played
a major role in the industrial explosion of postwar Japan,
until the debacle of the 1990s. The global economy, governmental corruption, an aging population, and economic
ballooning all contributed to the recent economic bust cycle
in Japan, but worker loyalty remained relatively intact.

Contrast the preceding with some disturbing trends in
the United States. Departments of personnel ("people")
have been replaced by departments of human resources
(equal to stocks of materials, somewhat like widgets, available when needed). Once the HMOs were allowed to kid-
nap the health and safety of our citizenry, they coined the
term "health provider," which encompassed every health
employee, from the neurosurgeon who operates on your
brain, to the physician's assistant who takes your weight
and your pulse, into the same package, thus saving bundles
of cash while driving future physicians into computer sciences. Some years ago, I discussed the managed-care situation with an executive of one of the leading health insurers
in the land. I was stunned to hear him casually comment
on the numbers of "lives" (rather than "clients") that were
under his company's control. This effrontery is now everyday parlance within the field. The Provider becomes stead-
ily and insidiously depersonalized.

Pitfalls and snares await the Provider during his vocational sojourn. The increasing role of women in the workplace, accompanied by their demands for equal, if not preferential, treatment, will be discussed in subsequent chapters. The older worker worries about job security, fears competition, and eschews change, which may well encourage resentment among his colleagues who are more expansively oriented. The middle-ager is concerned with his status, and must come to grips with the fact that his economic peak has probably been reached, and that his time for innovation has likely passed; while the younger employee is preoccupied with the possibility of effectuating change. The most frequently voiced concerns of polled employees were continuing health coverage, social security, failure to advance, how they would exist when retirement came, temporary layoffs, loss of jobs to the third world, and the realization that they were progressively losing the sharpness of their skills.

Add to the above the injection of ethical stresses and strains. Should a man lie when taking a series of psychological tests for a preferred position? Should the applicant admit to preferring *Playboy* or *Sports Illustrated* when he knows the company is looking for the *Reader's Digest* or *Forbes* type? If prostitutes are regularly procured by his competitors, ought he to follow suit and strain his marriage and his morals, or should he demur and risk both the loss of his job and the impoverishment of his family? If industrial espionage is thrust upon him, should he "go along" or inform the police? If his company blithely continues to produce a potentially dangerous product, as in the R. J. Reynolds tobacco case, what course should a man follow? Are his business dealings to reflect his personal morality, or should they approximate the ethics of a poker game? The answers only appear easy; living through the situation is an entirely different matter.

While these considerations are built into the occupational structure, the personality of the individual Provider is infused into the vocational blender, adding to the rise of psychological disabilities. Character traits have been held responsible for 90 percent of the causes of firings and 76 percent of the rationale behind refused promotions by one major company. The personality makeup is involved in numerous occupational syndromes and neuroses. Emotional illness is felt to cause at least 25 to 35 percent of work absences. As of 1997, consumption of alcohol constituted the nation's most common drug abuse problem. Alcoholism is found in well over two million workers, with an average of four to five missed weeks of work per alcoholic employee. Impulsive character traits account for a large share of accidents. "Low back syndromes" and compensation neuroses are often associated with depressions and feelings of persecution. The adage that these are "not cured until the 'green poultice' [financial compensation] has been applied" is too often too true. Supervisors become anxious, depressed, and tend to develop psychosomatic complaints due to responsibility and role conflicts. Paranoid traits among workers' representatives may produce morale problems and unnecessary work stoppages.

In the more creatively oriented occupations, the Provider faces the problem of work inhibition, in which, regardless of the heroism of his endeavors, his creative juices become dried up. One of the better known work inhibitions is "writer's block." A heretofore successful playwright was unable to complete the final act of a play scheduled for rehearsal in the immediate future. On approaching the typewriter, his mind simply went blank, for no ostensible reason. On investigation, it was soon obvious that his hostility toward his ex-wife was even more devastating than he had realized, and, unfortunately, his ex-spouse would reap a substantial windfall if the play proved to be a hit. While he was chopping firewood at a vacation cabin, a friendly psychiatrist advised him to envision his ex-wife's head atop each log. His energies waxed vigorous and fierce, and he exulted in every blessed moment of it. The last act was promptly completed, and the production ran for a full season on Broadway. Incidentally, the play's ingenue subsequently went on to achieve stardom, and became the recipient of an Oscar for best actress. The author died in 1997, but, nonetheless, thank you, Sammy . . .

In a yesterday that seems a million years ago, the Provider reaped more than monetary compensation from his labors. He could take pride in the products of his craftsmanship, and paternally pass the lore inherited from his father on to his offspring. His business was within a reasonable distance from his home, so that his activities were seen, understood, and appreciated by his kin and kith. The modern-day Provider, on the other hand, is employed in vocations that are often beyond the ken of his family. Try explaining the deft social dance of the account executive, and the intricacies of international arbitrage and offshore banking, to a young son. Furthermore, the Provider has become a phantasmal transient who arrives home after intolerable hours spent on some commuter conveyance, haggard and wanting only peace and quiet, hardly fit for even conversation with a spouse and children hungry for interaction with him. But the treadmill keeps running, and the Provider must keep apace.

Somewhere in this favored and affluent land there are men who look forward to Monday mornings, and who derive satisfaction and stimulation from their occupational endeavors, but there are many more who don't. Many of these denizens of the "world of the ulcer and the coronary" find it difficult or "unmanly" to admit to their dissatisfactions, anxieties, and stresses, for the Provider image is deemed intrinsic to their masculinity. As a consequence, their sufferings are accentuated and remedial action is inhibited. The Provider's woeful workhorse theme has been too passively accepted by generations of men. Responsibility, in its deepest sense, is met by a man adapting his vocation to his life, and not vice versa. Achieving this balance might start liberating the man.

4

The Sex Life of a Penis

The Disenfranchised Phallus

The sexual chronicle of the twentieth century is no longer simply an account of how often how many vaginas have played hostess to how many penises. The crux of the revolution it reports is the increasing respect accorded to the female sexual drive and the consequent backlash directed at male sexuality generally and the penis more specifically. The sweeping change from the antediluvian notion that "ladies lie still" to the contemporary feminist frenzy for more bumptious orgasms is as emancipatory in scope as was the Magna Carta. It has certainly penetrated more people than did that princely concession. College dormitories now invite coeducational cohabitation, virginity has become a questionable virtue, and varied versions of a feminine

Declaration of Independence have become enshrined in a deluge of books, periodicals, films, and the like. All that remains is the dénouement, its inevitable integration into our cultural thought and institutions. The exhilaration and the ecstasy of the bold challenge eases into pedestrian practicality.

Every upheaval, like every election, has its winners and its losers, the victors and the casualties. The sexual rights, and perhaps even the erotic supremacy, of women are presently in the ascendancy, and the clitoris will never again be regarded as a second-class phallus. The orgastic potential of women is now scientifically proclaimed as unquestionably more profound than the male's. Caricatured as a piddling appendage attached to a chauvinist male, the horn of the unicorn has finally acquiesced to the lotus blossom.

But every successful revolt creates its dispossessed. Adam after Eden, Napoleon at Elba, Newt Gingrich: what is the lot of the disinherited? The phallus appears as a principal casualty of our most recent social upheaval. Stranded by the Mystique's phallocentric propaganda, its heroic pretensions reduced to human proportions, the phallus has become a fallen champion. The disenfranchised penis emerges as the prototypic antihero who must deny in order to survive.

Under the aegis of the Mystique, the penis was placed on a superhuman pedestal, deified and adulated throughout the centuries. The Hindu god Siva was proclaimed the possessor of a phallus of infinite size by Vishnu and Brahma. Some trendsetter! Oriental art, particularly Japanese woodprints, traditionally portrayed the phallus as having dimensions equivalent to a man's other extremities.

The Greeks referred to the male sexual organ as *aidoion,* the inspirer of holy awe, while the Romans used its representations to decorate their homes and constructed mighty stone phalluses to delineate land boundaries. Early church fathers celebrated the fertile phallus by ornamenting church property with its replicas, while some African tribes collected the phalluses of their foes rather than their heads.

While this attention and flattery had its seductive aspects, it contained the germ of the eventual fall of the penis. How, after all, does one live up to the infinite? Being human is difficult enough: assuming a godlike posture brings down deific wrath. Hubris, that aroma of arrogance exuding from excessive pride, was the downfall of many a figure in mythology. It has also resulted in chronic downwardness of number of disillusioned penises.

One of the more trenchant observations of the erotic was W. C. Fields's "There may be some things better than sex, and some things may be worse, but there is nothing exactly like it." In truth, it is a unique experience. While other biologic drives, such as hunger, thirst, and elimination, are life-sustaining, have immediacy attached to them, and are essentially solitary enterprises, man's sexual impulse can be indefinitely postponed or even entirely eschewed, and is generally performed in concert with another human being. The consequent plasticity of the slowly evolving sexual drive allows a culture to more deeply permeate it and to mold it in accordance with whatever social relationships the society has opted for. The aim of man's sexuality is a pleasant activity, his society determines the ground rules of the game.

The two principal varieties of erotic experience are recreational sex and relational sex. The sex life of the penis reflects this duality, consisting of a nucleus of the recreational, surrounded by a host of relational elements that can either expand or devour it. A venerable psychiatric adage advises that a man has two heads, and when he uses both at the same time, he's in for trouble. The head between the legs is the recreational seat, while the head between the ears houses the relational. A well-made sexual cocktail is a fusion of these two elements, consisting of a recreational base, to which a jigger or two of the relational has been added, depending on one's taste. Too much of the additive indicates a poorly mixed and stifling concoction that a gentleman should return to the bartender. It has been the unhappy fate of the contemporary male and his well-intentioned phallus that his sexual center has been insidiously forced upward from the crotch toward the brain.

Recreational sex is experienced as enjoyable play, happily hedonistic, and emphasizes the sensate response of the participants. A phallic frolic, it is of no cosmic import, and free of compulsivity, imperatives, and guilt. It can be identified by such adjectives as "lusty," "earthy," "sensual," "voluptuous," and dozens of other intriguing terms that have unfortunately acquired a pejorative connotation in a togetherness-centered culture that is committed to the containment of recreational sex. How refreshing it is then to note the contemporary institutionalization of the term "friendly fuck," which connotes the serendipitous coupling of two old-time friends or ex-lovers for occasional leisurely episodes of the enjoyment of each other, just for the hell of it, or just for old times' sake, rather than for the evolution of society.

Society's vendetta against pornography is a case in point. Pornography is usually defined as material designed to appeal to the "prurient interest," to produce erotic arousal while "devoid of any redeeming social value." Apparently society cannot tolerate specifically sexual play, naked and uncamouflaged, and divorced from any social commitment or relational obligations. Yet pornography is far more beneficial to the individual than it is harmful. For those pornophiles who enjoy literary (remember James Joyce's *Ulysses?*) or cinematic titillation, it supplies an enjoyable though innocent sensual excitation, which normally pales if overdone. Men and women viewing films of repeated sexual intercourse generally become bored after twenty minutes or so. Members of the Kinsey Institute estimate that one out of three rented videotapes are X-rated, while their 1984 polling indicated that more than half the population of Indiana over the age of eighteen had watched pornographic films.

From the standpoint of the pornophile, adult pornography provides a multitude of blessings. It provides diversion and pleasure; it acts as a transient sexual stimulant, more effectively than alcohol or marijuana; it serves an educational function, bridging the gaps that parents and schools find difficult to fill; it encourages variety and experimentation, often a welcome addition to stultified sexual lives; and provides a masturbatory outlet both for the average male and for those who might destructively act out their antisocial sexual impulses. Pornophiles, as a group, are usually sensitive people with a capacity for fantasy, both estimable traits.

Pornography does have its share of problems however:

children as either participants or viewers; the exploitation and denigration of women; porno addicts; and exploitative rotters on the production side of the camera. The utilization of children in any sexual production, such as magazines or movies, is obviously criminal, and the miscreants involved should be sent to Siberia or worse. Parents should do their best to exert some supervision over their children, but this is a wide, wide Internetted world. Certainly some pornography is wretchedly demeaning of women, but, with rare exceptions, these are adult women who do elect to participate, and they have the option to move to other pastures, and their audience is always free to watch a quiz show instead. The sleaze on the production and distribution side of porno films exists, partially due to its having been socially marginalized. While those who are exploitative rotters are deserving of society's scorn, are they so much worse than those who buy and sell legislative influence and degrade democracy by transforming it into a kleptocracy? Finally, those addicted to watching pornography, like those addicted to spending their waking lives on the Internet, need some therapeutic intervention to nudge them into participating in the real world.

Relational sex, moving from the sensate to the cerebrate, places the emphasis primarily upon the "meaning" of a sexual activity as it relates to another person, institution, or entity. The relational factor adds a grab-bag element to a man's sexual responses. A cooperating brain may provide a positive reinforcement to the penis, with the addition of affection, fantasy, and active engagement with one's partner in an exploratory adventure designed to increase the genital response. But brains aren't necessarily cooperative. They contain the debris of early childhood misunderstandings and mishandlings; they have been exposed to the machinations of the Mystique and other forms of antisexual conditioning; they are often stuffed with imperatives, the "shouldn'ts," the "ought-tos," the guilts, and the assorted hang-ups that have been the lot of "civilized" man for centuries. Brains deal not only with the penis, but also with dimly understood archetypal parents, the injunctions of the church and the law. When cerebral compromises are effectuated between these protagonists, it is frequently the penis that pays the price. The brain may be a noble organ, but it is sexually unreliable.

Recreational sex ruled the roost until a few centuries ago. In the good old days, open sexuality was fairly commonplace, allowing for a generous genital fulfillment for both men and women. Public nudity, nonvirginity, pre- and extramarital dalliance was assumed, since sex was regarded as just another bodily appetite, like eating and drinking, and was unencumbered with lifelong emotional and legal commitments. The ancient Hebrews, primarily concerned with family and parenthood, placed no proscriptions against premarital sex in the Old Testament, and barely tolerated perpetual virginity in the Talmud. The Egyptians countenanced incest, expected women to partake in the initiation of amorous activities, and not only decorated their temples with explicitly sexual motifs, but supplied their dead with pornography and dildos to amuse themselves with as well. Sparta encouraged nude public dancing between youths of both sexes, and the ensuing sexual freedom was not unexpected. Nor was Athens noted for its sexual restraint. Religious festivals were associated with

socially sanctioned promiscuity, and the hetaerae, the acme
of Greek courtesanship, enjoyed a higher social standing
than most Greek matrons. At the height of the Roman
Empire, with marriage distinctly regarded as a political and
economic institution, sexual activity continued to be more
recreational and less institutional. This general state of affairs continued through the Dark Ages, until the twelfth
century gave rise to the medieval church and the ideal of
courtly or romantic love.

From its inception, the Christian church conducted a
crusade against the flesh and the Devil by extolling celi-
bacy, virginity, and self-denial. Christ lauded "those which
have made themselves eunuchs for the kingdom of heaven's
sake." Even marital relations were accepted only with great
reluctance. In the Epistle to the Corinthians, Saint Paul
advises: "It is good for a man not to touch a woman. Nevertheless, to avoid fornication, let every man have his own
wife, and let every woman have her own husband . . . I say
therefore to the unmarried and widows, it is good for them
if they abide even as I. But if they cannot contain, let them
marry, for it is better to marry than to burn." The church
fathers believed that the passions of this world distracted
men from the Paradise of the next, and that the suppression
of the bodily was the strongest inducement to the devotion
to the heavenly. As the church's intrusion into the bedroom
progressed, increasing injunctions were leveled against full
sexual expression, with imperatives toward self-control
pushed further and further. "The" position to be used in
coitus, and the hours of the day in which this might take
place, were prescribed. When the medieval church developed in power and prestige, matters became so gruesome

that marital relations were illegal for 203 days per year. Sundays, Wednesdays, and Fridays, plus forty days before Easter and forty days prior to Christmas, were declared sexless by some divine fiat. During this period of acute sexual repression, flagellation, hysteria, witchcraft, stigmatae, and other socially sanctioned forms of madness replaced calmer sexual sporting.

The ideal of courtly or romantic love grew with the development of the medieval church. Men were encouraged to adore an ideal, untouchable woman rather than to romp with a real one. Many commentators attribute the birth of the romantic ideal to the emerging veneration of Mary. When, in 1937, Havelock Ellis wrote, "The sexual embrace can only be compared with music and with prayer," he was merely giving voice to a twentieth-century version of the sanctification of the relational element in the sexual process initiated during the Middle Ages.

The penis continued to prevail under obviously adverse circumstances. Despite its physical limitations, regardless of conflicting messages from testes, cerebrum, and God, it gave a visceral performance. For once, the Mystique had come to man's assistance. Labeling him an Olympian Sexual Athlete who performed feats of wonder and awe, the Mystique concocted this penile placebo, a sugar-coated illusion calculated to provide a harassed athlete with that second wind enabling him to exert extra effort to convert the expectable performance into the unforgettable moment. But the life span of any placebo is limited, and the past several decades have seen the Mystique, for once, mystified.

With the weight of current comparison of male and female sexual capacities tilting toward the female, and with feminist writers demeaning the masculine with such un-kindly cuts as, "Nature seems to him to have practiced a niggardly economy when she came to designing man, in contrast to the munificence she lavished on the making of the woman," the penis has struggled valiantly to retain its integrity and self-esteem. It is little wonder that more than a few have retired from the fray, hors de combat.

The current sexual tide has produced swells of sexual talk and has resulted in more women becoming more in-sistent on deriving more sexual gratification. In fact, the crescendo is mounting to such a pitch that the quest for the orgiastic orgasm, or even multiple orgasms, no longer suffices. Germaine Greer, for example, exhorts women to "hold out not just for orgasm, but for ecstasy." If only she had defined her term! The obsessional component inherent in these endeavors is projected onto the penis as an in-creased demand for greater production from women who have already been informed that their capacities are all but limitless. Unfortunately, these exhortations neatly blend into the penile illusions fostered by the Mystique.

The contemporary penis finds itself the focal point of converging imperatives. The feminist call for infinite erotic fulfillment collides with its finite physical capacities; the echoes of the Mystique's evocation of the Sexual Athlete abut against inclinations toward being human; and testic-ular urges for the recreational contrast with the brain's em-phasis on the relational. Few, if any, organs function well in a conflictual environment, and the penis is no exception. A clarifying question might then be: "What can a man reasonably ask of his penis, and vice versa?"

The Average Expectable Penis

The penis is a rather remarkable instrument that houses three functions, procreation, recreation, and urination, in one small but expansive container. Women are more generously endowed with several organs to perform the same functions. Their vagina and uterus procreate, the urethra urinates, and the clitoris is there just for fun.

From the anatomical and physiological standpoints, we probably understand more about the functioning of the penis than we do about most other organs in the body. Its central canal, the urethra, is partly surrounded by spongy cavernous tissue that simply engorges with blood during sexual arousal, enlarging the penis from its resting three-and-a-half or four-inch length to an erectile size of approximately six inches. The increase in the blood supply that accomplishes this feat is primarily mediated by nerves emerging from the sacral (lower) segment of the spinal cord, responding either to reflex stimulation from nerve endings in the penis or to cerebral excitation that travels down the length of the spinal cord to activate these sacral neurons. Once stimulated, these nerve endings release nitric oxide, which allows smooth muscles to relax, and open the cavernous spaces, allowing the entry of blood, with erection as the happy consequence. The early stage of excitation results in erection, some elevations of the testicles, and a flushing of the chest and neck. As excitation increases, a plateau stage is reached, during which the testicles enlarge some 50 percent, and a feeling of orgastic inevitability is

experienced. Finally orgasm occurs, during which everything at first seems to expand, and then contract. The
glands (prostate and seminal vesicles), the sphincter
muscles (urethral and anal), the urethra, and the penis all
spastically contract, ejaculation occurs, and the penis subsequently eases into the resolution phase, in which all elements revert to their normal conditions and proportions.
The penis becomes refractory to further excitation for varying periods of time, depending on one's age, physical condition, and degree of satiation.

It is the good fortune of women, who have their own
version of these stages, that they possess a negligible refractory period. They are able to effortlessly shuttle from
orgasm to plateau, and back to orgasm, until a state of
physical exhaustion is reached. While the average male is
spent after one, or a splendid second orgasm, per sexual
congress, a woman may have six or sixty orgasms, should
she be so inclined and enjoy the requisite physical stamina.
This has been somewhat disconcerting even to those penises that are able to maintain their erectile state for many
moments beyond the usual two to five minutes that the
ordinary male member remains within the vaginal vault before that final spasm. Once again, the good performance
cannot compete with the infinite, and intimations of inadequacy seep into the sensitivities of even the most prolific
of phalluses. The physiological fact of relative orgastic limitations has become the Waterloo of stoutly held pretensions of penile supremacy. To give the penis its due,
however, it must be recognized that the male and female
sexual responses are no more comparable than an aged
Scotch and a fine wine. Male sexuality is characterized by

a greater immediacy and urgency, while that of the female is more involved with a gradual summation and extended capacity. Both satisfy, but each in its unique way.

Although the male ego has been coerced by the compulsion to acquire plaudits for facility between the bedsheets, and lives in horror of inadequacy or aberration, there are simply no valid criteria for the "normal" or "average" penile performance. Changing times and customs, alterations in desires and demands throughout one's life span, make such judgments impossible. Statistics may tell us the average penile size, but there are normal variations that have little to do with the adequacy of function, since the vagina obligingly expands to nestle about whatever dimensions its entrant possesses. Since the vast majority of a woman's sexually responsive nerve endings are concentrated at her periphery (the clitoris, the outer third of the vagina and its surrounding tissues), depth of penetration is rather academic. Kinsey found that 77 percent of men were sexually aroused by observing pictures of sexual activity. Are the other 23 percent therefore "abnormal"? To respond affirmatively would only confuse "average" with "normalcy."

Similarly, the current statistical approach has the unfortunate side effect of emphasizing quantity (how frequent and for how long) over quality (how satisfying). However, the question "How normal am I?" hovers, like some spectral apparition, over the relationship between the man and his member, and therefore, should at least be addressed. Again, these should be considered but approximate parameters, extracted from reasonably reliable studies, rather than absolutes, engraved in stone, to be taken as gospel for each individual man. For the record, some of these sources are:

the University of Chicago, the University of Medicine and Dentistry of New Jersey, the Massachusetts Male Aging Study, the National Institutes of Health, et al.

The sexual landscape portrays the average man as having 59.1 episodes of intercourse in 1998, compared to 65.3 such encounters in 1996. Married men in the eighteen-to-twenty-nine age range had 116 conjugal episodes per year, while 17 percent of adult men reported no intercourse at all in 1998. The average man had 12.4 partners since age eighteen, while 17 percent had participated in sex for sale. Additionally, more than 25 percent of men have had at least one sexual experience with another man in their teen or adult years.

Mining the landscape, one finds a plethora of problems just beneath the surface. Significant "sexual problems" are reported by 43 percent of women and 31 percent of men. "Erectile dysfunction" (inability to achieve or maintain an erection for satisfactory intercourse, i.e., impotency) occurs, to some degree, in 30 percent of men, while 34.8 percent of men in the forty-to-seventy age range had moderate to complete erectile dysfunction. It has been labeled as an important public health problem by a National Institutes of Health Consensus Panel. It is worthy of note that, with a deterioration in economic security, the gamut of sexual dysfunctions occur in women, while only erectile dysfunction occurs in men. Interestingly, while sexual problems diminish with age in women, they significantly increase in the aging male. Add to the above that male victims of adult-child contact, and men who have assaulted women sexually, are similarly three times as likely to develop erectile dysfunction. Make of this what you will.

Premature ejaculation (when ejaculation occurs too soon, or before one wills it) is reported by 21 percent of men. Male college graduates are one-third less likely than the average male to experience premature ejaculation, but, curiously, men with liberal attitudes about sex are approximately 1.75 times as likely to ejaculate too soon. Men reporting any same-sex activity are more than twice as likely to experience an early ejaculation, as are the victims of adult-child experience. Apparently, diminished quality of life is to be found more among the impotently afflicted than among the premature ejaculators. Speculate to your heart's content, but don't bet on your conclusions . . .

Let's play. The average male in his twenties averages 2.6 sexual experiences (intercourse, masturbation, petting) per week. Let's assume that he confines these to intercourse, and is a reasonably facile performer, with each experience lasting approximately twenty minutes from foreplay to finale. He spends more time watching climactic commercials on television than he spends climaxing with his beloved in bed. By the time he reaches his forties, this statistic is reduced to 1.2 weekly coital connections. He spends more time shaving than he does copulating. Has the American male become repressed and desexualized? Or is sex just another of many biologic activities that has its limited appetite? Have our cultural distortions created a sexual never-never land in which man's penile expectations are inveigled to extend far beyond his biologic propensities? Or are all three true?

Apparently, most penises are disinclined to quantitative heroics, but the question of reasonable expectations still remains. Perhaps a consensus would agree to the following:

the adequate penis is capable of erection, and will enlarge given sufficient stimulation. It welcomes the company of women, or men, if so programmed, and shrinks neither from a partner nor from the prospect of active sexual engagement. It has the requisite flexibility to adapt to most of the brain's exigencies so that the enjoyable moments can be reasonably lengthened. It functions better in a warm and affectionate milieu than in a detached, hostile, or punitive one. It operates, preferentially, spontaneously rather than being driven by obsessive ideas or compulsive rituals. Finally, the penis that fits these criteria will be regarded as a friendly organ of pleasure rather than an intransigent foe by its possessor. Should a man's sexual functioning fall within this happy framework, any addenda are just so much icing on the cake, be the frosting variations of oral-genital divertissement, a festive orgiastic fantasy, masturbation, or copulating while standing on one's head. Variety not only spices up one's life, it acts as a penile tonic as well.

The Penis Under Siege

Contrary to the proclamations of the Mystique, male sexuality is a fragile entity easily disrupted by childhood psychic mishandling and readily turned off by slight misadventures, a word, a gesture, or a hint of fatigue. From the functional standpoint, the penis is probably man's most vulnerable organ. Impotency, fetishism, transvestitism, exhibitionism, and pedophilia are all but exclusively male phenomena. Homosexuality is thought to be at least twice as common in men as in women, and a premature orgasm, the bête noire of so many men, is nonexistent in women. The average penis partakes in some ten thousand orgasms during its lifetime. It is remarkable that so many function so well.

The brain has been increasingly referred to as man's true sexual organ since it has the capability of exercising an absolute veto power over penile activity. With this Damoclean sword constantly hanging over its head, with unconscious fears and inhibitions as ever-present potential explosive charges, it is understandable that the penis may view itself as under a chronic state of siege.

A dramatic demonstration of the besieged penis took place in Singapore, during an epidemic outbreak of Koro in the 1960s.

The male afflicted with Koro is gripped by the conviction that his penis is shrinking back into his abdomen, an unfortunate circumstance that will deprive him not only of his manhood, but of his life as well, since death is assumed to coincide with this occurrence. This belief is shared by family and friends, who frantically seek medical attention for the afflicted penis. The spectacle of frenzied and desperate men, their penises grasped in their fists or fixed with ribbons tied tightly around their legs, or fastened to boxes or weights, is horrendous to contemplate. During this particular outbreak, the populace somehow implicated pork as a causative agent, and pork dealers consequently shut down and silently stole out of town in fear of reprisal.

Medical opinion considers Koro to be a state of acute anxiety, precipitated by culturally determined fears of sexual overindulgence, which is generally, but not necessarily, limited to Southeast Asia, the Chinese province of Canton, and the Malay archipelago. The Koro syndrome provides an excellent example of the smooth cooperation among cultural, familial, and individual psychopathologies to place the penis literally under siege. Incidentally, there was not one recorded case of any penis becoming lost in the dark recesses of anyone's abdomen. Most men recovered with appropriate psychiatric treatment, although many retained traces of their former anxiety. Western culture has had its manifestations of Koro, though its onslaught against the penis is less literal and therefore less appreciated.

While the penis is beset by a conglomeration of inimical ideas, it is simultaneously threatened by the all-too-real world of bugs (spirochetes, bacteria, viruses), invidious organisms hovering about, just waiting to sink their teeth into it in the form of sexually transmitted diseases. From AIDS through to genital herpes, they are too often too lightly considered, and their dire consequences are tragically dealt with after the fact. The penis has every right to demand that its possessor use his reason, acquire the appropriate knowledge, and take the necessary precautions to avoid the unnecessary risk. Information can be gained from pamphlets, from health professionals, from friends, and from the media. Above all, one should get to know one's partner as well as one can before bedding her, or him. Very transient contacts have produced all-too-permanent illnesses. The relative comfort that safe sex and condom use affords can more than compensate for the minor inconvenience. While it is admittedly difficult to cover all the bases, life does go on, and sexual hypochondriasis should not remove the player from the ballgame. But it does add additional stress to an already burdened penis.

Men handle stress by adopting one of four basic techniques. Ideally, they utilize their rationality and modify, or adapt to, the provocative situation. Should this approach be unattainable, they either assume the offense, take flight, or attempt to circumvent the problem. Their penises function in a similar fashion.

Given the existence of a sexual problem, the knowledge and understanding of it often allows for a reasonably satisfactory solution. Adjustments can be made for misconceptions, irrational guilt feelings, and other oppressions. Should reason fail, the penis may be compelled to utilize one or several of the unconsciously motivated remaining alternatives.

It can preempt or attack—premature ejaculation—hit, run, and out; and quickly retire from the fray.

It can withdraw—into apathy or impotency, utilizing the bedroom as a four-walled arena to act out nonsexual needs such as dependency or power drives.

Finally, it can attempt to circumvent the conflict by changing its goal or direction, fixing instead on a deviation such as exhibitionism, fetishism, or sadomasochism, or perhaps adopting a homosexual or pseudohomosexual stance.

These last three options often place a man at odds with his sexuality, as if he were divided above and below the navel, with the two halves at war with each other.

The preemptive approach may produce such opposite extremes as Don Juanism and premature ejaculation. As a soldier may take a rashly heroic action to disprove his cowardice and fears, so may the sexually insecure male become a Don Juan to disprove inadequacy. The current fad of "sperming" by adolescents, in which they inject their sperm into the maximum number of girls, keeping score all the while, supposedly provides them with machismic medallions, presumably certifies their masculine prowess, and simultaneously insures against any presumption of inadequacy. The process is compulsive and never-ending; the next woman can always attest to the accuracy of his fear. Since the goal of his endeavors is unprovable, male-female interrelatedness becomes inconsequential and remains so as long as he pursues his quest.

Premature ejaculation, experienced by more than one-fifth of men, is that unhappy condition in which the penis climaxes before the brain has given its assent. It is sometimes misdiagnosed by the male since, unless ejaculation occurs at the moment of insertion or within three or four thrusts, the "prematurity" may depend on the alacrity of his partner's satiatory capacities. More than a few men have deemed themselves "premature" after thirty to forty-five minutes of penile thrusting into their partner's unresponsive vaginas. A sorry state indeed. The penis performed, but the brain was unappreciative. Given a more reactive or less frigid female, the question of their adequacy would not arise. But the present-day responsibility of the male to satisfy places the onus upon him, and perspective fades.

Some men have sought solace in Kinsey's thesis, which regards rapid ejaculation as a "superior" response, equating any rapid action in living organisms as ipso facto evidence of a desirable property. If this superiority thesis is valid, why don't women share in this blessing, or are we still dealing with the issue of feminine inferiority? Furthermore, why should masturbation be less quicksilver than coitus? Let us eschew any hint of male chauvinism and accept the fact that the too rapidly responsive penis is more often the result of male anxiety, specifically referential to women. Premature ejaculation is never experienced during masturbation, and it is an almost unheard-of complaint among homosexuals. It is an exclusively male complaint, since most women, if they do climax before their obliging partner, remain capable and happy to continue until their male companion's satisfaction is assured.

Habitual prematurity is the cry of a distressed penis, and its possessor should seek professional aid rather than Kinsey's questionable solicitude.

Hosts of beleaguered penises have defensively sought asylum in apathy. It appears that the male's emotional estrangement from the erotic is assuming protean proportions. It is becoming increasingly common to hear women complain of the sexual coldness and distance of their mates. In a typical survey of college-educated young wives, 25 percent complained of the infrequency of their marital relations. The fact that one in four women, at least in this survey, found their mates relatively disinterested in sex is no small complaint, and echoes what most psychiatrists are hearing in their consultation rooms. Penile performance is apparently becoming more perfunctory, along with a diminution in sperm counts. It is a moot point to what extent these complaints are due to Eve's seeking an ecstatic return to a more amorous Eden, or how much they are attributable to a general overwhelming of the male psyche. Probably both are true. Increased female expectations and demands are countered by increased indifference and detachment, the opening gambits in the apathetic alternative. The emphasis on "cool" and avoidance of sexual and parental responsibility promulgated by the contemporary youth culture has encouraged distancing. One finds the apathetic penis among young men who, although they may "sperm," are divorced from involvement and affection. As they age, partake in sequential affairs, or finally marry, their sex lives tend to become mechanized, devoid of variation, surprise, or innovation. Saturday-night genital approximations, ritualized pelvic motions, become as routinized as taking the 7:10 commuter train on Monday morning. Stimulation becomes a dim memory of things past, occasionally revived by a lithesome secretary or by a flirtatious gesture emanating from someone else's wife. The recreational penis now becomes preoccupied with urination. The fact that men and women were neither destined nor effectively programmed for a monogamous existence is lost sight of by a social order that fosters the myth of "and they lived happily ever after." As monotony envelops monogamy, both partners slowly drift apart toward the opposite sides of the bed. Passionate play, in some respects, is not unlike a football game. The same play, repeated over and over again, results in an impregnable defense. The constant invention of new plays, or a successful and well-timed mix of the old, adds to a team's variety, and increases its scoring potential.

The vulnerability of the male member is most graphically demonstrated by its withdrawal into perpetual detumescence. Impotency is the state of the ostensibly palsied penis, which cannot erect or sufficiently maintain an erection to permit intercourse to occur. There is no commandment that a penis must perform each time, under all circumstances, with every female it happens to encounter. Most penises have their occasional understandable lapses, and so its anxious possessor should not diagnose impotency based on a single or occasional happenstance. It is habitual nonresponsiveness that is the hallmark of impotency. Interestingly, while "erectile dysfunction," to some significant degree, was reported by 30 percent of men in 1998, a 1970 poll conducted by a popular magazine, *Psychology Today,* reported more than one in three responding males having erectile difficulties. It is probably the case that erectile dysfunction is the least publicized epidemic in decades, despite Viagra advertising.

Impotency results from a multitude of factors, from the primarily organic to the primarily psychological. Increasing attention has lately been paid to the physical: hardening of the penile arteries, diabetes, thyroid insufficiency, and multiple sclerosis, to mention a few etiologic factors. Drugs and booze are lethal combinations to happy penile function. Shakespeare's observation that alcohol "provokes the desire, but takes away the performance" is as astute a medical observation as would be found in any textbook. Italian ladies of the Renaissance used a drug that dilated the pupils of their eyes, converting them into deep, darkened pools of passion. The potion was called "belladonna," since it made women more beautiful. Belladonna derivatives are found in many over-the-counter sedatives today, purchasable without a prescription. While they continue to exert their hypnotic effects, excess dosages may deflate sensitive penises. Other medications within the average medicine chest (e.g., antidepressants, antianxieties) may have depressant effects on the penis as well. Heroin is also noteworthy for making men less horny.

It had been thought that a low level of penile erectability was associated with a low level of testosterone in the blood, especially in older men. But this has so far proven to be one more blind alley, for the therapeutic administration of testosterone usually has little or no effect on the impotent member. Some male homosexuals with low testosterone levels are exceedingly sexually active, with no erectile difficulties. Apparently, the penis requires only a minimal amount of the hormone for successful operation, and the somewhat lower levels in older men may indicate little more than sexual apathy, a lack of opportunity, or the absence of a stimulating and available partner.

Psychologically induced impotency is a problem-solving device employed by the brain to the chagrin of the penis. A physically incapacitated phallus never erects. The erection during sleep, the hard-on while awakening, the retention of a masturbatory capability, or the presence of an enlarging phallus with women other than the accustomed one all point to a problem residing above the neck rather than below the navel.

The havoc within the copulaphobic male arises from sets of conflicting themes. Exaggerated images of masculinity meet expectations of limited capacities; conscious desire for female contact conflicts with hidden hostility toward, or fear of, one, some, or all women; antisexual childhood conditioning confronts the erotic imperatives of adulthood; the search for physical pleasure abuts against imagined fears of punishment and genital injury. The themes are legion but, with the penis remaining limp, the anxiety-laden copulation is avoided.

Project yourself. After months of hesitation, and definitive workups by internists and urologists, you finally find yourself in Dr. Freud's office. Fidgeting in your chair, you confront a reasonably pleasant and interested man, not quite the stereotype you've seen in cartoons, who asks what the problem is. How does one express the problem? "I seem to have developed some sexual inadequacy." No. It sounds too technical, too impersonal. "I can't seem to get it up the way I used to." Again, no. It has a crass ring to it, too flip. "If I get a hard-on, I lose it before . . ." You begin to feel a bit ridiculous. "Look, I've become impotent." There, it's out, and he doesn't appear noticeably shocked or taken aback. Why should he, he's been hearing it often enough.

"When did it start?"

"I'm not really sure. I know that I've been less interested in sex for some time, but I dismissed it as a passing phase. And then it just seemed to happen. At first I couldn't hold an erection, and then I couldn't have one at all."

"At all?"

"Not quite. I frequently wake up with an erection, and I can masturbate, but when I get into bed with her, no dice."

"How do you feel about it?"

Somehow you hadn't anticipated that question. Your first reaction is distress and devastation. You're impotent, you're ashamed, you're incapacitated and functionally crippled, and yet all of you, to be truthful, isn't unhappy about it. There is a feeling of relief, a relaxation of pressure.

As treatment progresses, you find that you aren't a self-pitying, whining Alexander Portnoy, but simply a man using a symptom, impotency, to express "I've had it!" Striving toward a chimera of success for insufficient reasons, bored with a demanding wife or lover you've become emotionally estranged from years ago, feeling yourself aging and wasting your allotted time with little in the way of satisfaction, you have symbolically copped out. No more performing, you're crippled. "Don't expect too much from me, I'm limited." In one fell swoop you have expressed your rage, and reduced the demands. Small wonder that part of you secretly cherishes and clings to the symptom.

Prognostically, your chances of recovery are quite good. A change in the way you conceptualize yourself and the rest of your world may be called for, but the odds are that you will end up happier, and hopefully so will your lady friend.

Sex may become a vehicle for the expression of hostility, with each penile thrust regarded as an assaultive "fuck you." Some men are at their coital best only after a battle with their partner, with what passes for "sexual" activity serving as the final round of the fight. Rape, that supposed epitome of male lust, is ofttimes more an attack, albeit one that happens to be enacted within the sexual sphere, by men who are plagued by their own sexual inadequacies. As previously noted, men who have sexually assaulted women are 300 percent more likely to manifest erectile dysfunction. A pretty twenty-year-old teacher in a suburban public school was forced from her classroom at knifepoint by an intruder who had only moments ago robbed another female teacher. The attacker demanded money. When she showed him her empty purse, he abducted and raped her, his penis symbolically stabbing her again and again, in frustrated fury. The motive was attack, the tool was his penis.

The drive for power and control too often converts the playground of the bed into a phantasmal battlefield. "Good grief, I can actually turn her on!" is incredulously perceived by insecure men impressed and overwhelmed by the awesome power inherent in actually affecting another human being. Men who turn limp at the sight of their partner happily hovering over them in bed are generally men who have been more concerned with the affirmation of their own power and control than with sexual delectation. Fellatio, instead of being regarded as a sexual aperitif, becomes stimulating only by virtue of assumed female submissiveness and the complementary cunnilingus is shunned lest it connote male submissiveness. Prior to the sexual revolution, it was by no means uncommon for women to manipulate their men by granting or withholding sexual favors. Its popular translation was: "If he doesn't come across, I don't come across." With the sexual pendulum swinging in the opposite direction, men are beginning to use the same device, to the frustration of their frantic wives or girlfriends.

When a man's early sexual development has been so devastated that future sexual contacts are perceived sufficiently threatening, he may unconsciously but understandably develop a sexually deviant orientation. Exhibitionism, fetishism, transvestitism, sadomasochism, bestiality, and pedophilia are some of the possibilities. Some homosexuality might also be considered within this framework.

Through these deviations, the psyche attempts to preserve some measure of sexual gratification, while evading the fantasied specter of frightening consequences (castration, annihilation, and other such unpleasantries) attendant to the more conventional coital activities. While these "alternatives" are a commentary on the male's sexual fragility, they are also a tribute to his adaptive potentials. Residing almost exclusively within the male domain, they are seldom found in women, whose sexuality appears to be founded on sterner foundations. Kinsey reported only two or three female fetishists, no female exhibitionists (those who impulsively display their genitals to the opposite sex and derive sexual gratification therefrom), and only one-third the percentage of sadomasochistic responses when compared with male reactions. And these "paraphilias" (Greek *para* means "beyond," and *philia* means "love") only scratch the surface. Other variations abound, in nature and in intensity.

While the uterus and vagina relax, contemplating their creative potentials, the deviant phallus portrays the pounded boxer, the pugilist on the ropes, battered and covering up, weaving and dodging the real and imagined blows raining in upon him. Above all, he must avoid his adversary. And so the fetishistic phallus is aroused by inanimate objects (shoes, clothing) or by only a part of the body (feet, toes). "Fetishism" is derived from the Portuguese *fettico*, a charm, with the penis responding to the amulet, to a symbol rather than a real person. The transvestite achieves gratification simply from wearing female attire and makeup, as if a woman's dress will disguise the existence of a penis, thus warding off some dire genital threat. While women in drag may derive some satisfaction in male mimicry, a penile fantasy is not involved, and they seldom, if ever, become orgastic because of their attire. The masochist confronts the imagined assault in a more direct fashion, by symbolically incorporating the anticipated punishment for sexual pleasure into the act itself. In a sense, the masochist preempts the executioner by accepting punishment in advance, thus allowing orgasm to take place. Leopold von Sacher-Masoch, a nineteenth-century Austrian novelist, would entreat his wife, Wanda, to whip and to beat him as a prelude to sexual relations. Wanda courteously obliged, and Sacher-Masoch was immortalized in the term "masochism," or the more colloquial "S and M," as the epitome of suffering and humiliation in the pursuit of sexual gratification. Men have extended this bizarre erotic passion play to the point of deliberately placing themselves in life-threatening situations, with nooses tied around their necks, passively submitting to being burned with lighted cigarettes, or being beaten with metal clothes hangers to the point of unconsciousness. Others have pushed the play too far, ending up on a slab in the morgue rather than in some erotic ecstasy.

The Once and Future Penis

Proclamations announcing the permanent demise of the penis as a power within the arena of sexual politics may yet prove to be premature. While the penile position is apparently at its nadir, its capacity to adapt to changing circumstances has been evidenced in the past. A phoenix rising from its ashes, an Arthur who once was, and in the future will again be, "hic jacet penis, Rex quondam Rexque futurus," the phallic comeback is eagerly awaited by a generation of perplexed males, and by more than a few women as well.

The restoration of the penis to a respectable social position will require an innovative sexual renaissance that reaches beyond the instruction manuals and somber manifestos to the realm of relaxation and humor. The currently enshrined sacred cows, the cult of erotic aestheticism, the "equality" of male and female sexuality, the masculine role of initiation and technical proficiency, the female's right to define the male as a success or a failure as a sensual animal all call for a quizzical wink.

While other bodily functions have little in the way of the mystical attached to them, human sexuality has been accorded a unique distinction. The Olympian heights of relational sex, represented as a divine spasm in which the human race transcends itself, is beyond the capacities and aspirations of many an adequate penis. Let's redefine sex on a more physiological and less spiritual level, as a shared playful escapade rather than a transcendental experience of "Beauty" and "Sanctity." Social groups that are relatively free of this "spiritual" aura regard sex as a natural process, no more aesthetic than any other bodily function. Sexual intertwinings, couplings, and contortions are exciting and pleasurable, but describing them, or the intensely felt summation of stimuli, as aesthetically beautiful or spiritually significant would appear to be semantic acrobatics. The freedom to be simply and unencumberedly sensual is the least the penis can ask of society.

A gentle reappraisal of the male role in sexual relations would be appreciated by most penises. The assumption is made that the male is always sexually available, his penis aching to become erect on a moment's notice with but the slightest provocation; that he should and will restrain himself as long as his mate deems it necessary; and that he will somehow induce the orgasm to which his partner, in her current state of enlightenment, is unquestionably entitled. There is a pervasive inequity in this arrangement. The onus placed upon the male is vast, while the female's responsibilities are relatively minimal. One survey of sex manuals indicated that men were the recipients of three to four times as many instructions as were women. It would seem that these eroticized versions of *Popular Mechanics* were geared to the production of computerized, automated phalluses, programmed to please their partners rather than to enhance their own responses, since the cock crows earlier than the hen. Women are consequently forced into the role of judges who define the success or failure of their male partners. Most studies show that some 30 percent of women are nonorgasmic via intercourse, and furthermore, with the exception of premature ejaculation, there is little clinical evidence that the man's technique, within the strictly coital framework, actually determines whether or not a woman reaches her moment of fruition. Cunnilingus, clitoral massage, anal play, and the current rage for the use of vibrators all help to salvage the reputation of the lover, and the penis is grateful for the respite.

I have listened to numerous men describing themselves perspiring in the all-too-common overly extended erotic embrace, their penises having despaired of the opportunity for a natural and spontaneous orgasm, their minds concentrating on multiplication tables or the horrors of the following day at the office to calm their insistent penises, mechanically thrusting in and out to induce their partners to finally utter that blessed word "come." Excitation gives way to mechanization, sex becomes work, and the high-spirited penis is dulled and dispassionate.

Men must transfer more responsibility to women for their own moments of ecstasy. It should be incumbent upon both men and women to communicate their sexual wants and preferences to their partner. What type of fore-play is most enjoyable? Should clitoral stimulation be direct or indirect? Do lingual, anal, or priapic stimulations turn her on or shut her off? How much intercourse does he or she prefer? If a woman's requirements are conveyed, and are congenial, it is only reasonable for the male to comply. Should her needs be unstated, insatiable, or subject to change without notice, the woman should have the fundamental humanity to accept the problem as her own and encourage her partner to cease his superhuman efforts and to comfortably and relaxedly ejaculate. Freed of the imperative to "satisfy" and more relaxed in its consequent performance, the penis should become more prolific and less prone to future potency problems. Indeed, the best insurance against impotency is an active sex life plus the availability of a physically and emotionally healthy partner.

The penile resurrection will regard the notion of sexual "equality" as both artificial and absurd. There are more inequitable situations in life than there are equitable ones, and the concept of "fairness" is more often honored in the breach than in the observance. There are differences in the sexual responsiveness of men and women, both individually and collectively. Tastes, expectations, and performances differ. The simultaneous orgasm has been established as the male's diploma, a certification that he has received his Ph.D. in Passionate Play. Yet simultaneity is by no means the norm, and, considering the difference in male and female responses, it might best be regarded as a pleasant artifact. Instead of the responsibility for sexual regulation and satisfaction devolving upon one partner, it should be a joint venture worked out as harmoniously and hedonistically as possible by both participants. Given a sufficiently adventuresome attitude, most men and women can experience more than a modicum of satiety without recourse to manuals or gurus of technique.

The male initiatory role must also be regarded as passé and quietly go the way of the mastodon. Why must the insecure male, or the man who is made anxious by assertive behavior, make each and every advance? A major technique employed by sex clinics, for example, has been the assigning of the initiatory role to women. They initiate foreplay; they straddle the male during intercourse, better controlling the action while taking greater responsibility for it; they squeeze the premature penis to control early ejaculation; they stroke and they fondle. Whatever degree of success sex clinics have achieved, the relaxation of imperative pressures upon the male must be given its share of credit. Historically, many cultures have found no difficulty in allowing for female initiatory behavior; why not encourage its normalcy within ours? It apparently has a beneficial effect on both sexes.

The concept of the impetuously erectile penis is an additional candidate for oblivion. While the seventeen- or eighteen-year-old penis is hot-blooded and likely to be on the move, it finds sex less immediate with age, and is content with fewer orgasms. Some men fear this normal change of pace as a reflection of diminished virility. Panic sets in and they become candidates for impotency or sexual apathy. They might better compare themselves with a veteran baseball pitcher who no longer relies simply on speed, but has become a master of pace and control; his wildness gone, he throws fewer but better placed pitches.

The epilogue to the saga of penile salvation can only be written when the penis is rescued from the Mystique. The Sexual Athlete has played overly long, and his contract should be terminated. Sex will then be recognized as amateur recreation rather than a crucible. If a man insists on "proving himself," let it be in an area other than the bedroom. With the decline of the Mystique's imperatives, with a bill of divorcement from grandiose penile pretensions, men will view their appendages in human terms, and so will women. Then let the games begin!

5

Hot Cockles and Husbands

Hot Cockles

Hot Cockles was a sixteenth-century English country game in which a blindfolded player tried to guess who hit him. It is currently being resurrected on a more sophisticated and psychic plane, with a significant crop of contemporary husbands and fathers serving as the befuddled man in the middle. Pelted on all sides by invidious insults and assaults, he often neither understands what is happening to him, nor knows where the next blow will originate. Lately men are hearing the more fractious of the feminist set define marriage as "hell," and many husbands who had assumed a lifetime of incomparable bliss now find themselves portrayed as Satans overseeing their demonic domains. Patriarchy is deemed paganism, housewifery is equated with slavery, and motherhood is pictured as some monstrous miasma into which the female has been forced by her surly spermatic spouse.

Unaware that covert but compelling forces are set on changing the rules of the marital game, these family men have blithely believed that what was good enough for their fathers was good enough for them. And why not? They were trained for it from infancy, and their Oedipus complexes were resolved by the determination to find a girl just like the girl that married dear old Dad. Somnambulating in their Provider roles and anchored to their Achiever Complexes, they seemed justified in their belief that women never had it so good. But, alas, times are changing. Consider, for example, the results of the Rutgers University National Marriage Project, released in 1999, which indicated that the nation's marriage rate had fallen by 43 percent in the last four decades—from 87.5 marriages per thousand unmarried women in 1960 to 49.7 marriages in 1996, the lowest in history, and that the percentage of couples who reported being "very happy" in marriage fell from 53.5 in 1973–1976 to 37.8 in 1996. A significant something's afoot.

Marriage evolved from a probable stratagem to preserve and protect the mother-child bond to a universal social institution designed to provide a congenial milieu for the maximal well-being of the individual, while insuring the maximal stability of the social order. It is a functional arrangement that offers an effective economic utilization and consumption of products, an assured sex life, and a manageable method for the generation, legitimization, and the rearing of offspring, despite Margaret Mead's musing that fathers are a biological necessity but a social accident.

Benjamin Franklin praised its practical utility in his *A Letter from Benjamin Franklin to a Young Friend on the Choice of a Mistress:* "It is the man and the woman united that makes the complete human being. Separate, she wants his force of body and strength of reason; he, her softness, sensibility, and acute discernment. Together they are more likely to succeed in the world. A single man has not nearly the value he would have in a state of union. He is an incomplete animal, he resembles the odd half of a pair of scissors. If you get a prudent, healthy wife, your industry in your profession, with her good economy, will be a fortune sufficient."

Aristotle viewed marriage and family as "an association established by nature for the supply of everyday wants." One might add that marriage also allows the fulfillment of a basic need that most individuals cannot fulfill for themselves: an ongoing intimate relationship with another person. At its best, it has served as the vehicle for that satisfaction of a host of dimly perceived needs as well, such as dependency, security, and self-esteem. In an increasingly impersonal society, there is a necessity for personal warmth and intimate relatedness. Although an admittedly imperfect instrument, marriage has remained the most rational physical, emotional, and pragmatic arrangement for most people in the ordering of their lives.

But with increased diffusion of social parameters, and the rise of the "me" generation, the institutions of marriage and the family have been put to the test and to the question. Marriage can be compared to a besieged fortress, with those outside the walls struggling to get in, while the defenders inside desperately pray to escape unscathed. The question is, "How is it faring?" Of course, occasional sorties against home and hearth are not new. Kate Millet's prediction that marriage will wither away, and Ms. Greer's carefree counsel to women to remain single are tepid puffs compared to August Strindberg's: "The Family! Home of all social evils, a charitable institution for indolent women, a prison workshop for the slaving breadwinner, and a hell for children." A veritable tsunami indeed, heralding the increasing frequency, popularity, and social acceptability of these critiques. A few examples: Ms. Balogan suggested that the personal relationships of marriage must undergo a revolution, with the eventual dissolution of marriage and the establishment of all-female communes to take its place. Her sagacity is exceeded only by the viability of her alternative. Ms. Linda Gordon proclaimed: "The nuclear family must be destroyed, and people must find better ways of living together." What better ways, given the complex society in which we live? Further mention of similar suggestions could go on ad infinitum, and sometimes ad nauseum, but the themes are repetitive, the solutions a tribute to obfuscation, and the husband all too often labeled "it" in this latest and perhaps most serious round of Hot Cockles.

However, nuptial blessedness is evidently currently suffering from a crisis of confidence. A cursory sketch of some variables may help concretize the parameters. From 1960 to 1996 the median age for women marrying for the first time increased by four and a half years, from 20.3 to 24.8. In 1960, 90 percent of women twenty and older had married, while this percentage had been reduced to 83 by 1996. Similarly, the numbers of never-married men doubled, from 7 to 15 percent, in the two decades from 1970 to 1990. While the divorce rate, which peaked in 1979, has settled down, one divorce does take place for every two marriages, and the twenty million currently divorced constitute nearly 10 percent of the adult population over eighteen. The family constellation has been similarly modified, with more families opting out of parenthood. While 44 percent of families were childless in 1970, since 1990 they have outnumbered those with children. Two-thirds of divorces involve children, and these innocents will inherit a greater propensity to be themselves divorced.

The preceding data have been interpreted as an invitation to hysterical imprecation by the connubial Cassandras. Amid the screeching, it is understandable that many husbands and fathers, feeling hustled and hot-cockled, wonder how it all came about.

The Blindfold

The motive forces behind marriage have ranged from the pragmatic to the romantic, from survival to "love." In simpler times, up to a century or two ago, the pragmatic was clearly and admittedly predominant. The complementarity of male and female roles added to the survival of each. The pioneering husband busted the sod and built the cabin, while his wife baked the bread and basted the buckskin. After an Eskimo bridegroom returned with his catch of caribou meat, his bride chewed his boots to prevent them from freezing and cracking, enabling her husband to brave the elements and resume the hunt on the following day. The Irish farmer, rooted in the soil, married only "when the land needed a woman." Since this need only arose when his mother could no longer perform her household chores, the average age of the rural Irish bridegroom hovered around thirty-eight. The land and its requirements were paramount, affection or romance were inconsequentials.

An extension of the survival motif was the derivation of physical and/or economic comfort from marriage. In 1596, Shakespeare wrote: "I come to wive it wealthily in Padua / If wealthily then happily in Padua." Three hundred and fifty-two years later, in 1948, Broadway audiences amusedly empathized when Cole Porter, appropriating this refreshing candor in *Kiss Me Kate,* added, "If my wife has a bag of gold / Do I care if the bag be old? / I've come to wive it wealthily in Padua." Perhaps times have not changed too much; the show's revival in 2000 still drew the same chuckles. The quintessential quid pro quo, this "you scratch my back and I'll scratch yours" unquestionably resulted in many workable, albeit businesslike marriages. Since prolonged proximity has been known to produce a passionate intimacy, many must have been hotly successful.

The survival functions were extended to include the welfare of the individual's family, relatives, or tribe. In these instances, the prospective spouses served as agents for their group, contracting economic, proprietary, and social alliances. While these contracts were primarily for the benefit of their kith and kin, the contractor partook in the multitude of benefits afforded. The arranged marriage may have had a paucity of passion, but settling within an extended family and a surety of permanence were not altogether unreasonable trade-offs. If romance developed subsequently, so much the better. Stars may not have veered from their orbits, emotional skyrockets may not have exploded, but marriage held firm, producing generation after generation. Matters might have been worse.

The rise of the romantic began in the nineteenth century, more distinctly in the Anglo-Saxon world, and most pronouncedly in the United States. By this time, the more primitive survival problems had either already been dealt with, or the responsibility for their solution had passed from the family domicile to the more dubious domain of society. Society implicitly pledged to a man the physical safety of himself and his family, the education of his children, the enrichment of his retirement years, and, in a burst of paternalistic enthusiasm, offered him access to the American Dream (whatever that may mean) and a bridge to the twenty-first century (wherever that be found). The functions of the family became shared with legislators, jurists, and a presumably benevolent bureaucracy.

The breakdown of the extended family (several related generations functioning as a single household and/or economic unit) was accelerated by the industrial and technologic revolutions. Urban anonymity produced alienated souls, shuttling between masses of people and isolated apartments. As men were increasingly impelled to establish roots in nuclear families of their own, they faced the problems inherent in a relatively closed dyadic relationship, without the benefits of the aid and input of ancillary members of an extended family. However, this was to be compensated for by the establishment of the affectionate marriage. With an assured sexual relationship serving as the pièce de résistance, affectionate marriage became a highly marketable commodity. It filled a need, had no competition, and seemed reasonably priced. Future customers were trained for it since childhood, and knew that they would face social disapprobation should they abstain from the transaction. The affectionate ideal cornered the matrimonial market. The practical had ceded to the romantic, hearts palpitated a wee bit faster, and lovers could be observed scattering into the sunsets.

But our enlightened society has developed a mania for merchandising. The marketing strategy for the affectionate relationship became "love." "Love and marriage" became as conjoined as the horse and carriage. "True love" was romanticized and sanctified in magazines, books, movies, and was invoked as the deus ex machina when things got a bit rough. Evidently, when "love" was here to stay, bills would get paid, interpersonal conflicts resolved, and, in making love not war, mankind seemed headed for a renegotiated lease on the Garden of Eden. "Love" became the raison d'être of marriage, and vice versa. The more mundane factors such as similar value systems and socioeconomic backgrounds, compatible levels of aspiration, and mutual respect took subsidiary roles to such adolescent jabberings as: "But we love each other, what more do we need?" The answer, in all likelihood, might be a good divorce lawyer.

A French proverb cautions: "Try to reason about love, and you will lose your reason." Any such discussion can be considered sacrilegious: i.e., exactly what is meant when one says "I love the Lord," and precisely what transpires when "the Lord loves me"? While "A Prisoner of Love" may sell more than a million records, a critic of love runs the risk of being vituperatively branded a misanthrope. Analyzing love, one is told, is like dissecting a frog to learn how it functions. You may expose the component organs, but in the end you are left with a dead frog. However, men have not only married and sacrificed for love, they have also perished in its name.

"Love" is a four-letter word that covers so much territory while defining so little that it has become all but devoid of semantic utility. While it may be the touchstone for the poet and the philosopher, it can be a psychiatrist's unending labyrinth. The Hanunoo of the Philippine Islands, a rice-growing society, have ninety-two words for "rice." Their stomachs and their economy depend on it. The Eskimos use at least eleven words for "snow." Its varied forms and textures have a life-and-death significance for them. Yet we have but one word for "love." I love my wife, and I love my children. I also love Peking duck, scuba diving, and the Marx Brothers. Love, it seems, has a ghostly quality. Everyone talks about it, but no one can pin it down. Voltaire agrees. "Love has various lodgings," he noted; "the same word does not always signify the same thing." It may have different meanings at different stages of one's life. John Ciardi observed that "Love is the word used to label the sexual excitement of the young, the habituation of the middle-aged, and the mutual dependency of the old."

Still, if "what the world needs now is love, sweet love," and since man will evidently persist in mouthing that which he cannot define, perhaps the following is at least a working concept. What we call "love" is basically a complex set of progressive bonding experiences, with both psychological and physiological correlates, that promotes a caring extension of one's psychological boundaries to incorporate another human being as a part of one's self. It involves the establishment of an ongoing mutual identity, providing a partner for the building and development of a chain of life experiences. The physiological aspect is exemplified by "mother love." Natural mothers generally do not actually bond with, or "love" their babies until birth, when the pituitary floods the maternal circulation with the "love hormone," oxytocin. The sight or cry of an infant stimulates the pituitary to increase oxytocin production, resulting in additional ejection of milk from the breast, and deepens the bonding between the mother and her child. One can assume that corollaries to this experience exist in adult "love"; if one "loves," one feels it. Certainly adoptive mothers develop it, for we all know adoptive mothers who are as fiercely maternal as any birth mother.

"Love" is to be distinguished from passions more limited in scope, such as affection, infatuation, and sexual romance. "Affection" is a "caring for" or warmth felt toward another person. It does not, however, involve the incorporation of the object of affection into one's psychological self. "Infatuation" is a transient, albeit ecstatic, reaction to an idealized image of the partner. "I met this perfectly wonderful girl in this totally fabulous place . . ." is a case in point. "Sexual romance" is the gilding of the glandular with an aura of the profound, another instance of relational sex being invoked to ennoble a genital excursion. When Robert

Graves defined love as "a universal migraine / a bright stain on the vision / Blotting out reason," I think that he was really defining sexual passion.

It appears that love has become an oversold and misunderstood element in marriage. Alone, it is insufficient; misinterpreted, it produces disappointment and disillusion. Unaccompanied by the cement of commonalities, marriage for "love" is a fragile entity, with the bridegroom having unwittingly purchased a ticket to a game of Hot Cockles.

The Players

Romantic rationalizations to the contrary, most marriages are arranged, not in heaven, but in the unconscious psyches of the participants. A man's unexplained intuitive feel is frequently more perceptive than his rationality. With all the world to choose from, the average man was more likely to marry a girl who lived within a half-mile radius of his parental home. The fact that he was most likely to meet someone who patronized the same store, church, or tavern is only a partial factor. The neighborhood girl was more likely to share his social, economic, and cultural background, as well as his expectations from marriage. Since she would probably come from the same ethnic stock, she might also remind him of his mother than would a strange girl from a strange city. The color of her hair and eyes, her figure, her voice and its inflections, are prone to call up associations of the women of his childhood, with their associated warmth and security. This feeling of familiarity, this meshing of similarities and complementarities, have been major determinants in the mating game, and add cohesion to marital stability.

But changes are occurring at warp speed. Couples are meeting through the Internet, in chat rooms, personal ads, and impersonal "meets" in office lobbies, department store escalators, and the like. Intermarriages between religions and races are becoming standard, but there is no reliable data regarding their stability or success. The possibilities are intriguing, but so are the problems. As an illustrative example: I had the opportunity to counsel upper socioeconomic professional Indian men, and their American girlfriends or lovers. The frequently found crux of their problems was that the men had been raised in India, almost exclusively by women who nurtured and catered to them, with little in the way of relationships with male peers, and that they carried these expectations into their subsequent relationships with the opposite sex. The women, on the other hand, were not geared to nurture, and expected more independence from their consort. Most of these relationships failed, resulting in some men returning to India for an arranged marriage, in which both husband and bride understood their predestined roles. It is noteworthy that the divorce rate in India is a scant 2 percent.

Few, if any, marriages are devoid of their unconscious deals and fantasies, with their evocation of power, dependency, and other nuances that were implanted from infancy onward. Some men unknowingly marry to create a private empire to rule, in contrast to the impotence they may have experienced in childhood or as adults. Many men, inept in the world of their peers, behave as tyrants at home, inviting enmity from their families in place of affection. An only child, accustomed to being the sun about whom the planets revolve, may bring similar expectations into his marriage, demanding a perpetual kowtow from the wife and kiddies. An oldest child, with his predilection for performance, may assume a somber, caretaking role in wedlock, while a youngest son might envision marriage as a game in which he is perpetually nurtured and applauded. Should wifely responses to any of these types be other than compliance, awe, passivity, or approval, Hot Cockles may lurk in the wings. The variations are manifold, but since the game is played on an unconscious level, our player is generally blindfolded and unknowing.

It may be of solace to the cockled gamesman to appreciate that women are subject to similar unconscious drives, fantasies, and disappointments, which are invested with their own sets of rules and experiences. Fortunately, people tend to zero in on those whose personalities and needs best nestle with their own. Perhaps this is the major factor in the phenomenon of the long-lived marriage.

The Changing Game

As the societal core has dramatically altered within the past quarter century, the marital and the familial have been correspondingly reshaped. From economic cooperation to romantic union, from serial monogamy to cohabitation, from male-female dyad to domestic partnership, that most intimate of adult relationships has been swamped by changes too vast and too rapid to be reasonably assimilated. The "value" systems of the day before yesterday seem numbed or transmuted; i.e., extramarital sex and premarital pregnancy are now assumed, while divorce has become just another rite of passage. An era of impermanence and immediacy, the rapidly disposable combined with a reduced tolerance for "working things through," has left an indelible stamp on all relationships. Familial ties have loosened, and more and more family jewels are on display in pawnshop windows.

The increased power and independence of women exemplified by the feminist movement, the woman's control of contraception and pregnancy, and her remarkable incursions into the economic realms, have increasingly tilted the power relationships in marriage toward the wife. In *The Decline of Males*, Lionel Tiger noted that the typical family of the mid-fifties consisted of a working breadwinning father, the maternal house-bound housewife, and the several kids. It described 60 percent of American families. That 60 percent has now been cut to 4 (sic), an astonishing figure, with the working wife now contributing 40 percent of the family income, and one-third of these women earning even more than do their husbands. At the same time, the average man of the house faces increased instability. With the social contract between employer and employee rapidly dissolving, he faces increased job insecurity, questionable certainty of benefits, downsizing, and a more grueling lifestyle with increased time devoted to work. Additionally, there has risen the specter of the commuting father, who has less hours to spend with the family, thus impairing his son's ability to identify with him, and increasing the probability of both excessive dependency and delinquency in the boy. The traditional family dinner, where the various members dined together, exchanging ideas and experiences, has gone the way of the twenty-five-cent hot dog. This mutual conclave has been replaced by individual take-out meals, eaten haphazardly and in solitude, in front of television sets portraying caricatured family situations in which parents are harebrained half-wits and children are the repository of wisdom. Fathers, in particular, are presented as lovable boobs and hapless innocents who are extricated from ludicrous gaffes by their frequently silly but worldly-wise wives. A laudable example to present to children each evening. Parents and their children become increasingly estranged from each other, and the schism between generations widens. Amid those islands of isolation, grandparents find themselves divorced from functional utility, except for occasional baby-sitting, and eventually migrate to Florida or other "retirement villages" to await death in the sunshine.

This indelicate shredding of the social fabric has both contributed to and highlighted what may prove to be the most critical issue of our time: the validity and continuance of intrahuman bonding and the future form of emotional linkages. Is the lasting emotional bond passé, dysfunctional and anachronistic, or should men fight like hell to keep and to strengthen it? Are permanent male-female relationships the "closed-dyad disease," or are they the most reasonable alternative to a lifelong series of passing bumps, a series of inconsequential caroms from one person to the next, relatively devoid of significance? Has humanity finally progressed from the Age of the Home to the Era of the Motel? If so, what are the consequences?

A rapidly rising alternative to the conventional marriage is the increasing incidence and acceptability of cohabitation (unmarried couples who live together). From 1.5 percent of households in 1977 (1.1 million) to 4.8 percent in 1997 (4.9 million), this variant of family life deserves serious consideration. A current study reported by the Institute for Social Research at the University of Michigan states that 56 percent of all marriages between 1990 and 1994 were preceded by cohabitation, up from the figure of 10 percent in the years 1965 to 1974, and that while 55 percent of cohabiters eventually marry each other, 40 percent of these later divorce. Still, better than average. While 40 percent of children will spend some time living with their mother and her unmarried partner, the consensus among sociologists is that the greater instability and discontent in these generally short-lived relationships does not bode well for a child's future adjustment in his or her marital relationship. We can only speculate about the impact of cohabitation. Is it an omen of a significant development in dyadic relationships, or should it be considered as a transient living arrangement that some people find more congenial? If some people find commitment a hindrance, why not? But if this be the case, should they have children? How significant will this be for the future of the "family"? We can only speculate.

The case against the family portrays a harassed husband tied by legal thongs to his bored and infantilized spouse, a sorry being who has sacrificed her claim to personhood to the stereotyped mediocrity of child-rearing and homemaking and she becomes a candidate for an extra-marital fling or depression when the nest has become emptied of its fledglings. Locked into an unnatural monogamy, a statistical freak in the history of humankind's arrangements, the two turn inward, wrenching a semblance of support from each other under the guise of a legislated and sanctified togetherness. This closed unit acts as fertile soil for the germination of jealousy and possessiveness, in which privacy, separateness, and extrafamilial emotional contacts are looked upon as disruptive and "disloyal." The children of this happy union are portrayed as hapless victims of oppression and domination by parents who visit their own neuroses on their progeny, thereby generating and further perpetuating humanity's slide into a neurotic netherworld. The maternal complaint bemoans the woeful effect that kiddies have on sex and marriage, the restrictions placed on the mother's freedom, and the fatigue involved in child-rearing, with its ennui, its anxieties, and the wretched inconvenience of it all. Boredom and fatigue are either to be eliminated from our vocabulary, or become neatly encapsulated within the wonderful workaday world of men. In like fashion, "fatherhood" is surely the greatest folly since Seward's. Since fathers see less of their children, who cost more to raise, and provide greater headaches with fewer satisfactions, the male opting for fatherhood must be either insane or inane.

Defenders of the family, if they possess a minimum of honesty and good sense, admit to the partial validity of these charges, although they may detect a hint of caricature in them. The defender's ultimate response is a "Yes, but . . . what is the alternative?" Civilization, to survive, must be pragmatic, and, as yet, no alternative systems less imperfect than the family have been offered. Cohabitation is still up for grabs. The basic human needs, security, commitment, intimacy, interdependency, and the humanizing effects of child-rearing, are seldom to be found outside the permanent bonds of the family. How many men can claim they have reaped these benefits from a series of revolving-door relationships? Admittedly, monogamy is an artificial device fostered by society to insure its stability. But even among the more gonadally propelled men I have known, after a while faces blur, one crotch begins to resemble another, and the gyrations of last week's partner become indistinguishable from tonight's, and the majority reach a point where they would happily trade the fling for the familiar, the chimera of the chase for the actuality of devotion.

A stable civilization requires a stable citizenry, and vice versa. The universal parental function has been the preparation of the offspring to survive as independent adults. This preparation occurs best in what Heinz Hartmann referred to as the "average expectable environment," a milieu characterized by reasonable limits, expectations, and predictable responses from the important people in a child's environment. If he did A, he could count on receiving B. If he was helpful, for example, he could expect praise, while if he was disruptive, he would expect a reprimand, consistently. If the environment becomes unpredictable, if the child meets with unanticipated reactions, anxiety and instability eventuate. In this admittedly ideal family setting, a child develops security and rationality that he will subsequently convey to his society. Where can this milieu be better assembled than in a family structure? Sequential parents, one-parent families, or parents abandoning their parental roles to schools, peer groups, and the like, will not suffice. We would face generations of children who grow as weeds, untended, uncared for, and uncultivated, devoid of reliable standards. Granted, parenting has become progresively difficult. With the current social tumult, a father frequently finds himself bewildered, not only as to what the future environment will be for his offspring, but also as to current norms. What does a father tell his daughter, for example, about premarital virginity? His gut reaction might be to say, "Keep it, hold onto it," but is this really to her benefit? And since she will probably marry in her mid-twenties, might not premarital sexuality enhance both her life and her marriage? How honest, forthright, and assertive should he advise his son to be in the vocational rat race? Should he promote or discourage aggressive behavior in his progeny, when their society is becoming increasingly predatory? In the past, responses to these and other such questions seemed pat, standard, and constant. But sure responses have been shattered, and it is only the courageous, interested, and involved parent who will come to grips with them, earn the respect and affection of his children, and exact the joys of parenting, which have become so chic to deride.

In the midst of the deluge stands the husband, lately profaned and defamed. He has already made his investment, based on good faith and centuries of human experience, but the bottom seems uncertain. Has he been foolish or farsighted, coerced or courageous? The answer will remain vague while the current innings of Hot Cockles are being played.

Pitfalls and Penalties

Hot Cockles reaches its peak intensity during divorce, with the courtroom serving as an oak-paneled arena. At the docket stand the 1.1 million men who are divorced each year, with an equivalent number loosening up in the bullpen, taking the prescribed and ritualized steps prepatory to their day in Splitsville. The old saying that you never know your wife until you see her in a divorce court is, of course, true, with more and more women initiating the proceedings. Facing the presiding judge, the average divorcing male is prone to hallucinate. He imagines a black-robed avenging angel, sternly preparing an emotional and financial guillotine, for when the legal machinations have run their course, the cockled gamesman will feel himself severed from his habitual way of life and from his wallet. Frequently, he will not understand why.

A column in the *New York Times* entitled "I Am One Man, Hurt," tragically underlined the dismal point. Writing under a pseudonym, the author informed us that he was in the process of being divorced, but "I don't want to be, I am horrified at the prospect, I think it is the most devastating thing that could happen to my family, but it is going to take place. My wife wants it." How did it come to pass? "I thought we were a perfectly happy family until my wife told me, without any advance warning, that she

didn't love me anymore and wanted a divorce. Not a matter
of infidelity or alcoholism or beatings or arguments or desertion, but that didn't mean anything to her anymore and
she wanted out." The author's understandable agony, an
increasing commonplace, ends with the despairing cry of
the archetypal protagonist of Hot Cockles: "I am one man,
hurt, groping. I do not have the answers to the most important questions in my life. But I think for the good of all
of us, as a people and as a society, we had better start
coming up with better ones than we have now." Amen.

Unless the divorcing man has his next inamorata waiting in the courthouse corridor, he will likely emerge somewhat stunned, feeling alone in a world of singles, torn by
feelings of guilt, failure, and anger. The mystical oneness
is split in twain, the partnership is now a solo enterprise,
and his other self has become an alien and avaricious entity.
Estrangement from his children, a nightmare, becomes
progressively more vivid. Bizarrely, 38 percent of men paying child support are granted neither visitation nor custo-
dial rights. Inexorably, the "high cost of leaving" seeps into
his consciousnes. It is not unusual for a man to watch with
amazement while one-third to one-half of his after-tax income evaporates in alimony and child support, horren-
dously excoriating his meager standard of living and
labeling him a financial cripple to any of the female sex
who might consider him a reasonable risk for a subsequent
matrimonial adventure. After the legal fees, child support,
division of property, and adagios with the Internal Revenue
Service, the severing male conceives of himself as an
economic eunuch, normal in appearance, but functionally
sterile.

His erstwhile spouse, now socially saddled by her children, financially fettered, and facing a lonely and uncertain future, understandably feels sorely used and embittered. In 1998 there were more divorced women (11.1 million) than men (8.3 million), since women are less likely to remarry. Should she reenter the dating rat race, she perceives herself as dehumanized, fair game for philandering husbands, and just another slab on a never-ending meat rack. Her antagonism toward her ex escalates, and the friendliest and most civil of divorces tends to sour. Some divorcées devote the remainder of their lives to a vendetta against their onetime love, choosing vengeance over sanity, and often wreck both lives in the process. One woman, terminally ill, announced that she refused to die as long as her ex was sending alimony checks. It probably prolonged her life. Previous comfortings are replaced by mutual cruelties, and the embattled participants become too preoccupied with venom to understand.

When the legal lacerations have stopped bleeding, the cockled combatant might reflect on the hows and whys of the wreckage, conducting a psychological postmortem upon the corpse. People seldom divorce with conscious awareness of precisely what went wrong. They dissolve out of desperation and disappointment, out of a concatenation of feelings that, having been left unattended to fester, finally cry out for separation rather than repair and reconciliation.

The divorces of the past were more cut-and-dried, and readily identifiable in their causation. Callous cruelty, drunkenness, desertion, and uncontrolled lechery were sufficient and understandable. Divorce proceedings resembled morality plays in which evil was confronted by good, was adjudged at fault, and received its just and proper punishment. But in these less moralistic times, no-fault divorce has arrived, and rightfully so. While those baser and more blatant justifications still exist for uncoupling, psychiatrists and lawyers are increasingly dealing with divorce situations stemming from a new discordancy, in which a previously stable and fairly harmonious equilibrium had somehow grown dissonant. More attempts are being made to ascertain the sources of the splitting, to rectify them if possible, or at least to prevent their repetition the next time around.

Upsurgences of discordancy have both intrapsychic and circumstantial origins. The former would include the psychological patterns and problems of the participants, the fantasies versus the realities of their marriage, and the congruity of their meshing; while the latter encompasses the sociologic milieu and unforeseen circumstances that may impinge on the best of complex and long-standing relationships. The exigencies of life may upset the best of intentions. Financial incapacities and reverses, in-law problems, the strains and disappointments associated with fertility/infertility workups, the birth of children with significant mental or physical incapacities, chronic illness, and the like, can add a sufficiently high stress factor to crumble a reasonably well constructed home.

The intrapsychic factors, however, are attaining their share of the limelight, as testified to by the increased amount of space devoted to them in the popular press and magazines. All individuals have their neurotic quirks and patterns that they bring to a marriage along with their hygienic habits and table manners. Marital proximity focuses and often accelerates these traits, either to the betterment or detriment of the relationship. The spouse who flies high wedded to a partner whose feet are firmly fixed on earth, or the intellectual espoused to an emotional respondent, may produce very workable partnerships. Sadists and masochists make excellent mates, as do alcoholics and martyrs, and machismic males and dependent females. They fit. As long as each continues in his or her prescribed role, the relationship blossoms. Should one partner change, however, through growth, fatigue, or just becoming fed up, the equilibrium is unsettled and dissolution looms.

Other matched peculiarities may not be so fortuitous, however. While optimists will invest much of themselves in a marriage, the more pessimistically inclined will close themselves off and invite separation. Obsessive-compulsiveness, which initially produced the happy homemaker, eventually produced the carping pain-in-the-neck insisting that everything be exactly in its place. Paranoid traits, often associated with pathological jealousy, have served as excellent catalysts for divorce. The associated excessive suspicion and mistrust tend to increase after the ceremony, terminating in unanswerable charges and accusations against the innocent spouse, who, unless delighting in masochism, will proffer charges of his own via a divorce attorney. One such situation brought back memories of a decades-old drama, *The Shrike*, with a strikingly similar plotline. Barely three months after the wedding ceremony, a wife bizarrely planned to produce a "nervous breakdown" in her spouse, to have him hospitalized, and "cured" of his imagined philandering. She would then take him home, broken and subdued, but never daring to even think of another woman again. Happily, he became aware of her pathology and the ensuing divorce saved his sanity.

The fantasies of, and the act of, marriage are seldom totally congruent. When they are sufficiently divergent, the reality is rendered unlivable, even among the best intentioned. Some women, from the Barbie doll stage onward, immerse themselves in richly romanticized fantasies, from the cute "meet" through the "whirlwind courtship" to the final "I do"—and there the fantasy abruptly ends. The actualities of the day-to-day living with a man were never seriously considered or anticipated. Tempers and toilet paper, dishes and diapers, the unappreciated gesture and the unshaven husband, come as shockingly alien concepts. Numerous women complain of sexual frigidity occurring shortly after marriage, despite the swingingly orgiastic premarital relationships they enjoyed with their husbands-to-be. Once the romantic weekend trysts give way to the sanctioned reality, they close up and freeze up. Early demands for separation or divorce are a surprise only to their husbands.

Similarly, a man might visualize marriage as merely an addition of a permanent Bunny to his Playboy pad, a lithesome testimony to his masculinity. After the hippety-hopping has run its course, and the plaything asserts her personhood, the questions of responsibility, relatedness, and family arise, and the pad may be perceived as a prison to escape from.

The variants are many. Among those inwardly convinced of their unacceptability, the "if you really love me, you'll accept me at my worst" gambit may be employed.

Its practitioners unwittingly test the affections of their spouse by presenting themselves at their worst, with the hope that if the spouse sticks, they are somehow worthwhile and safe from desertion. The rub is that the only spouse who would stand for this ploy is either markedly self-effacing or masochistic. In the event that the partner refuses the test, the practitioner generally hears the worst detailed from the witness box. Or consider the man with the perpetually open mouth, waiting to be emotionally fed. He fantasizes marriage as a return to the womb, with his wife serving as a primordial mother, the source of an ever-flowing cornucopia of goodies with which she is to nurture and care for him. Should she slip, should a meal be delayed or one of his directives overlooked, the man-child reverts to childlike temper tantrums. The perpetual turbulence frequently terminates in divorce.

A major but insufficiently appreciated cause of marital disruption is the inability of one or both partners to adapt to the changes that are intrinsic to the maturation of a marriage. The typical marriage has its life cycle, with its sequence of stages, each of which evokes some degree of disequilibrium that necessitates readjustment and reintegration. The process might be compared to a steeplechase race, a zesty and challenging course with its sequence of hurdles and obstacles that must be perceived and gracefully overcome. A hurdle poorly managed or failed might permanently disqualify the contestant. He may opt out of steeplechasing forever, or try again with a new partner in another race. But it is the high hurdles of the steeplechase that capture the imagination and make or break a marriage.

The first and most hazardous hurdle is the postnuptial period. Here one confronts the fragmented prenuptial fantasies, the obviously erroneous mismatches, the too-hasty elopements, and the pathos of the person basically unsuited to an intimate relationship with another human. When one uses marriage to escape from the family homestead, the patterns of the past obtrude upon the present, unwanted and unwittingly, to the escapee's dissatisfaction and the spouse's consternation. It is by no means an easy jump, yet most make it and progress to the second, some two or three years away.

The second hurdle is reached with the birth of the first child, when the "couple" becomes the "family." The seven pounds of squalling protoplasm concretizes the marital commitment, and adds a new quota of contentments and complexities to the life of the couple. The husband must now accept the ceding of the center stage to the newcomer, a more difficult concession than is generally appreciated, while the wife must feel sufficiently competent to nurture, or to have the means to find sufficient help to enable her to do the job. In the era of the extended family, there was generally a plentitude of helpers to assist the fledgling mother, but in the more isolated nuclear family of today, this assistance is frequently absent and the maternal tenderfoot may feel chained to the bassinet and the sandbox, unappreciated by her husband. Furthermore, the couple must combat the jealousies, possessiveness, and the resurgencies of ancient sibling rivalries that the child evokes. Insecure mothers may resent a child's positive responses to his father as evidence of their own maternal inadequacy. The births of subsequent children bring additional pleasures and stresses, necessitating further adaptations within the family constellation. In one instance, a father who, as an oldest child, resented the births of his younger brothers, strongly identified with his first child and rejected his subsequent children. The consequent battles with his wife, with the drawing up of sides, all but dissolved the family until the issues were exposed and clarified within a therapeutic setting.

The third obstacle has lately been popularized and heightened by the efforts and writings of the feminologists. It coincides with the entry of the last child into school. No longer primarily preoccupied with child care, the wife, now approaching her forties, looks forward to the next forty years and wonders what they will be like. She has read articles and listened to lecturers inform her that her worthwhileness and individuality stem from her productivity outside the home, and that she unwisely sacrificed her personhood for her family. Perhaps it is not too late to rejoin the rest of humanity in its march to achieve. But her family functioning has left her vocationally crippled, or at least retarded, and now, no longer able to rely on child-rearing as her raison d'être, she may feel befuddled and lost, and look to her husband for support and reassurance. He, however, is having problems of his own. He is now in his early forties, the make-or-break years of his career. It is the beginning of his final push for position, and the call of the corporation frequently is heard above the distress of his wife and the cries of his children. Feeling adrift, more wives turn to alcohol or extramarital affairs at this point, for that final fling before menopause.

The fourth hurdle is reached when the youngest child

leaves home and enters the world outside, creating the now infamous "empty nest." The child-centeredness of the couple's past twenty years is now a collection of memories and old photographs, and the original pair is once again a twosome. But the couple has changed, jointly and individually. The husband, now in his late forties or early fifties, may feel himself closer to the end than to the beginning, with his best years, creatively and otherwise, behind him. His life's ambitions and aspirations are perceived as unrealized, and he must come to terms with this fact of his life. Having probably experienced occasional episodes of sexual dysfunction, he may feel his prowess waning, and be amenable to an extramarital fling for reassurance and rejuvenation. Should his penis perk up from the novelty, he might conclude his marriage to be faulty, dissolve it, and move into a September affair, attempting to begin anew. His wife, meanwhile, is coming to grips with her menopause, a seldom celebrated event, with whatever symbolic significance it has for her. In a situation that cries out for a renewal of contact, each partner may be too preoccupied with their own problems to be of much help to the other, i.e., the man could increasingly emphasize his mate's positives, while she could be more sexually inventive and reassuring. The tendency to look outside, to those ever-greener pastures, is often more tempting than a constructive gazing together at a mutual life to be lived and shared. The marked upsurgence of marital separations at this hurdle testifies to a series of failures and disillusionments, many of which could have been avoided.

While marriage has its singular joys and ecstatic moments, it should not be forgotten that strains, stresses, and problems are a normal and integral part of this ongoing process. There are times when a man must "ride it out" rather than ride away, and focus on the totality rather than the detail. When a normal stress is reacted to as a pathological plague, when outside or professional assistance is eschewed by a do-it-yourself mentality, unnecessary divorces take place, with their quota of misery, impoverishment, and heartbreak for the man, his wife, and his children.

Before the rash divorce, before opting for the heaviest game of Hot Cockles, a man and his spouse should attempt a rational assessment of the marriage. If there is a commonality of aims and objectives; a commitment to "making it work"; an emphasis on mutual enjoyment; a reasonable degree of sexual satisfaction; compatible value systems; and a bearable degree of reality stresses, the marriage should be fundamentally sound. If a man has a relationship of this quality and is still contemplating divorce, he should, at the least, seek a professional consultation first. He owes it to all concerned. Decreasing the immediate availablity of divorce, i.e., via "covenant marriage," tightening up grounds for divorce, and so forth, has both advantages and disadvantages. Each couple presents its unique situation. If, on the other hand, the balance sheet shows a severe deficit, a speedy disengagement might be called for, since many neuroses are kept hot and alive via pathological marriages. Getting out while the getting's good has preserved the property and sanity of many a cockled gamesman.

Instant Replay

Marriage is not a Shangri-la. Its capacity to serve as an oasis of affection and security is limited in a climate of tumultuous expectations. Rather than an insulated paradise, matrimony emerges as a complex processional, involving a host of unconscious interactions and, not uncommonly, the conflicting needs of the participants.

Disappointed by the absence of angels, some critics now trumpet visions of devils and damnation. While the predators gleefully pontificate on the imminent demise of marriage and the structured family, it might be appropriate for a few hardy souls to address themselves to the reaffirmation and reinforcement of marital bonding, to heal and construct rather than to destroy and to bury a viable patient.

Since marriage remains one of the most crucial moves and involvements in the lives of most people, it should receive at least as much attention in the schools as does trigonometry, French, or the *Canterbury Tales*. There should be mandatory formal education beginning in high school in the processes involved in mate selection and marital interactions. A student who learns to recite "amo, amas, amat," should also learn that there is more to marriage than romance. This sequence of courses might be included within the curriculum of the humanities or social sciences, and be conducted with the utilization of both formal lectures and seminar discussions. Since these are to be more than mere rap sessions, the instructors should have adequate training in dynamic psychology and in human relations, drawing upon psychology, sociology, and anthropology for primary source material. Topics such as the Masculine Mystique, matrimonial fantasies, and the role of one's past in marital reactivity would be included. Here, marriage might be divested of such myths as the "instant panacea" and "eternal undying love." Students might be advised to cultivate a well thought out program of mutual activities and interests with their future mates to prevent the growing apart that infests so many marriages. Didacticism does not change a psyche, but it might create a few mental pigeonholes, enabling one to stop and at least think, and to be more aware of what he's doing and perhaps have a hint of why he's doing it.

Some modifications in societal attitudes must be effected. The concept of marriage as a select and specialized institution, which no one must feel pressured to enter, should be encouraged. The bald fact is that many people are unsuited for even a moderately successful marriage. Let society recognize that no marriage is preferable to a bad marriage; the costs of the latter are too high. Consequently, any stigma should be removed from singlehood, just as the gay liberation movement has attacked the social stigma attached to homosexuality. Those who opt out of matrimony might choose any alternative lifestyle that harms no one, free of social disapprobation and social prejudice.

Premarital cohabitation should be encouraged rather than frowned upon. The adage that "you never know someone until you live with them" is more than folk knowledge, it is unvarnished truth. If marriage is to be strengthened, let's stop the mistakes early in the game, preferably before the nuptials. Since the vast, vast majority of engaged couples enjoy premarital sexual relations anyway, the likelihood of this suggestion fostering a re-creation of Sodom and Gomorrah is rather unlikely. This proposal might also allow postponing marriage until the couple is surer and more mature, help to keep the birth rate in check, and legitimize necessary and healthy sexual experimentation. Although 40 percent of premarital cohabiters eventually do divorce, at least their eyes were opened somewhat wider than the more conventional divorcers.

A campaign should be waged to resurrect the extended family system as a needed and healthy adjunct to the nuclear family. Greater efforts should be expended to bring grandparents back into the community, to increase their sense of participation, and to enhance their self-respect. With a greater sense of vitality and self-esteem, their contacts with their children and grandchildren might be enlivened, and the latter might be more ready to extract and utilize some of the wisdom accumulated by their elders during the span of a lifetime. Likewise, contacts with siblings, cousins, aunts, and uncles should be encouraged where possible, even by an occasional letter or telephone call where distance obtrudes, to enable the couple and their progeny to feel part of a network.

A man should know as much about the marital institution and the nature of his personal involvement as is humanly possible. Then, it is hoped he will become a referee rather than a participant in Hot Cockles, and the game might, in fact, be finally terminated as the sixteenth-century anachronism it really is.

6

The Gay Life: Fact and Fiction

Homosexuality is assuredly no advantage,
but it is nothing to be ashamed of.
—SIGMUND FREUD

You are attending a soirée in a parallel universe. Seated at one table is an odd sextet: Alexander the Great, Leonardo da Vinci, Julius Caesar, Plato, Tchaikovsky, and Cole Porter. A rather heterogeneous group; you wonder what they might conceivably have in common. The conversation is sparked by Leonardo ruefully reflecting on his imprisonment in Florence on charges of homosexuality, and Caesar complaining of his reputation as "the husband of every woman, and the wife of every man." Other dining companions with similar inclinations might include Michelangelo, Sappho, Marlowe, Noël Coward, and innumerable persons of talent and repute whose homosexual predilections have understandably been hidden in their respective closets. Since homosexuals have been beheaded, castrated, burned at the stake, imprisoned, disgraced, assaulted, blackmailed, and forced to suicide as a result of their supposed "crime against nature," the advertising of one's sexual "deviance" has appeared a gallant though rash enterprise. Since they are shunned and ostracized as social pariahs, it is small wonder that so little information has been gathered about the etiology and lifestyles of men and women whose sexual preferences are for those of their own sex.

However, homosexual men do occupy a significant area within the male landscape. Surveys from 1948 (Kinsey, et al.) through that of the Alan Guttmacher Institute in 1993 indicate that approximately 4 percent of American males lead exclusively homosexual lives. If we then include the additional 10 percent who have been exclusively homosexual for at least three years between their mid-teens and mid-fifties, this predominantly homosexual group would be large enough to populate Detroit, Philadelphia, Washington, D.C., Los Angeles, and a substantial assortment of other smaller cities. To further complicate matters, try to define the word "homosexual." Do a few same-sex encounters, or several homosexually tinged dreams or masturbatory fantasies definitively define the orientation? Forever? Must it include genital penetration of some sort, or is a kiss or a fondle sufficient? Should a man be exclusively heterosexual? Is bisexuality the biological norm, and the heterosexual just kidding himself? Is a man necessarily either-or? Kinsey and his group, in 1948, devised a seven-point scale, from 0 to 6, with 0 representing exclusive heterosexuality (activities, dreams, and fantasies all female directed) while 6 (the same dreams, fantasies, and actions all concerned with other men) denoted exclusive homosexuality. Nearly half of the males interviewed fell somewhere between these two extremes. Apparently, sexual orientation is a more fluid entity than appreciated by our cultural doyens. Pat Robertson and Jerry Falwell, where are you?

For simplicity's sake, the following might be an operating definition: let's use the term "homosexual" to refer to any adult who is predominantly aroused by, and/or who engages in repetitive sexual activities with, members of his or her own sex. This definition would exclude those who partake in "situational" homosexual activities, such as men in prisons, where heterosexual opportunities are not available. It would also exclude that cluster of men whose dependency and assertive needs compel them to identify with those perceived as more powerful and competent. Since they are basically frightened and insecure heterosexuals, eventually desirous of a successful relationship with women, they tend to rely on identification with other men to provide them with the wherewithal to succeed. Clinically, they might be considered "pseudohomosexuals." The man who is immersed in homoerotic fantasy, although sexually inactive, should be considered homosexual. The above definition excludes the concept of "latent homosexuality," which is an imprecise idea that has given far more confusion than aid.

But, putting exact definition aside, the gay liberation movement has increasingly become a force to be reckoned with within the last half century. Perhaps it began in 1935, with Freud's letter to an American mother who requested his assistance for her homosexual son. In his now famous reply, Freud wrote, in part, "Homosexuality is assuredly no advantage, but it is nothing to be ashamed of, no vice, no degradation . . ." This was then followed by academic studies such as Kinsey's, which exerted a demystifying influence. The rise in public concern over civil liberties, coupled with the revolution in sexual mores, focused further attention on the homosexual condition. Homosexual organizations, established in the 1950s, increased in numbers and in influence. The male Mattachine Society was incorporated in California in 1953. The name "Mattachine" was deliberately selected for its obscurity. The original Mattachines were professional entertainers and advisors to the Italian nobility notable for their truthful approach in the face of the unpleasant consequences that might ensue should their predictions prove faulty. The female counterpart of the Mattachine Society was the Daughters of Bilitis, "a woman's organization for the purpose of promoting the integration of the homosexual into society." The name is derived from *The Songs of Bilitis* by Pierre Louÿs, in which the supposedly heterosexual Bilitis becomes a disciple of Sappho and lesbian love. While the original purposes of these and similar organizations were to educate the public about homosexuality and to assist the adjustment of the homosexual within his society, they developed an understandable militancy as they evolved.

The homosexual counterpart of the Boston Tea Party was the Stonewall Rebellion. Police and legal harassment had been an onerous but tacitly "accepted" part of the life of the active homosexual. Raids on places of congregation, primarily "gay bars," had become an expected and wretched commonplace of existence. In June of 1969, a routine raid was visited upon the Stonewall Inn, a Greenwich Village bar frequented by a substantial homosexual clientele. Instead of the typically pacific parade into the waiting paddy wagons, the customers revolted, pelting the police with bottles, stones, and other missles. Police reinforcements were called and the riot quelled, but the issue had been joined. Various militant homosexual groups united under the banner of the Gay Liberation Front, and public action became the order of the day. The original educative and self-help activities directed at obtaining legal and social acceptance for homosexuals were replaced by demands for full equality with heterosexuals on a social and cultural basis, with the more radical of the groups promulgating homosexuality as not only an alternative but a "preferential" lifestyle.

The increased activity and visibility of the gay community has resulted in a corresponding increase in the public's curiosity about, and attempts to understand, the homosexual: the lifestyle, attitudes, how he might best fit into the community (i.e., with regard to the military, marriage, adoption, and so on), the issues of etiology and "abnormality," and the legitimacy or illegitimacy of homophobia.

The Gay Life

It may be presumptuous for a heterosexual to accurately describe the gay life, but it is also the case that each homosexual, like the blind man describing an elephant, has his own facet of the gay life with which he is most familiar. To begin with, there is no single gay style, but rather a spectrum of subcultures as one does find in the "straight" life. From the man quietly emerging from the closet, through to the flaming radicals flaunting their predilections in the Gay Pride parade, each man attempts to find his niche, depending on his personality makeup, luck, and the circumstances that his particular milieu affords.

Some, probably the minority, settle down permanently with one special partner, forming bonds that last a lifetime. Others find themselves ensconced within a congenial group, which affords a reasonable degree of caring and communality, and occasionally, a lover. The majority, however, cut off from the heterosexual world around them, frequently seek multiple relationships within a gay milieu in an effort to achieve a sense of belonging as well as the satisfaction of various emotional requisites. The popular conception of a pseudo male-female type of relationship does not generally stand up under scrutiny. While one partner is often dominant, there is more a sharing of congenial role activities in life, both in and out of bed. Unfortunately, unconscious or dimly perceived needs of the partners are infrequently met, and, consequently, the breakup of these partnerships is more often the rule than the exception. In those relationships in which one partner assumes the role of a substitute father or mother figure, the elusive tower of strength, understanding, and support is rarely equal to the assignment, and stormy dissolutions are not infrequent. There are those fortunate few who make the adjustment, and their accomplishment, under great societal pressures and disapproval, should not be lightly dismissed.

The majority of homosexuals find themselves in stressful and emotionally isolated life situations, as evidenced by their relatively high suicide rate. The common homosexual experience is the continual "cruise," a constant excursion into the world of gay bars, baths, and other public meeting places in which encounters occur, evaluations are made, and assignations established. Bars often specifically cater to particular clienteles, i.e., Sadie May (sado-masochistic), D/s (Dominance/submission), transvestite (although many transvestites are not necessarily homosexual), leather (for the motorcycling inclined). Dr. Evelyn Hooker, a psychologist who has extensively studied the homosexual population in California, described the gay bar as serving as "an induction, training, and integration center" for those entering the gay life. The habitués of these various establishments are quite eager and willing to initiate the homosexual tenderfoot into the rules of the game and the facts of homosexual life, hopefully including a lecture on AIDS and safe sex. They are instructed in the varieties of sexual activities, the wonders of the one-night or ten-minute stand in which a sexual relationship is deliberately transacted in an impersonal manner. Bodily contact without the pretense of interpersonal commitment or attachment is the rule. Person-to-person is replaced by genital-to-genital. Novices are taught the nuances of gesture, the eyeball-to-eyeball invitation, and special nonverbal communications that signal interest and availability. There is emphasis on youth, physical attractiveness, and "well-hung" genitals. Glibness and repartee replace deeper conversation. Of course, this is rather rough on the aging homosexual, whose physical and social attributes are no longer assets. If he has not settled into a permanent relationship, he becomes the exploited purchaser of sexual services who can no longer make i on his own. It is difficult not to sympathize with those homosexuals over forty, whose lives are less than half lived, and who find themselves sexually and socially over the hill. Or empathize with the older solitary male estranged from the one lifestyle that has offered him some degree of satisfaction, a lifestyle that has now paled into a jaded obsolescence from which he can seldom recover.

A case in point is this extract from an open letter published in *Gay Sunshine*, a San Francisco periodical: "I am forty-two years old. No, no—don't tell me it doesn't matter! It does, and you know it does . . . You know as well as I that the gay culture is youth oriented. Young guys go for young guys, and old guys go for young guys; and nobody goes for old guys. They don't even go for each other. What is the gay culture currently offering the middle-aged man? Voyeurism in the clubs? A twenty-buck hustler? Fawning sycophancy as a bar-fly auntie? No thanks! . . Isn't it ironic to go around carrying placards and giving speeches declaring 'I'm liberated, gay and proud of it!' and to go home and go to bed alone again? . . . It's just that I have been disappointed too often to continue, especially at my age, to hope that I will find what I have been searching for so long."

Moving on to the more extreme end of the spectrum, we confront the radical gay activists who, for personal and or organizational purposes, concentrate on grabbing society's attention, usually in an in-your-face fashion, and blatantly blasting a caricatured homosexual agenda. Typified by organizations such as Queer Nation, or by the more provocative elements in the Gay Pride parades, the radical participant flaunts his society, or his family, by bizarre exhibitionistic dress or by provocative challenging sloganeering. From the mild "Try it, you'll like it," or "Two, four, six, eight, being gay is better than being straight," to the counterproductive "Suck cock for Jesus," their message is seen and heard, although more often to the embarrassment of the other members of the gay community. In this classic example of a Pyrrhic victory, they gain their moment in the sun, but lose their supporters in the process, and blot out the constructive efforts of the Gay Men's Health Crisis and God's Love We Deliver. There is a distinction between raising a bit of hell for the constructive purpose of gaining attention to support a cause (e.g., AIDS, gay rights), which is quite reasonable, and the hurling of symbolic excrement, which is not only questionable but also counterproductive.

Why the apparent self-destructiveness? We all, hetero and homosexuals, develop defenses, and kid ourselves as to our true feelings about so many things, and then try to validate our lifestyles, for better or worse. I have found this to be particularly true with homosexuals I have known as friends and as patients. The following example may be illustrative: I was once taken by a Japanese colleague to a gay/transvestite private club in Tokyo, where we spent an extended evening with five Japanese transvestites, one of whom was a star in Japanese cinema, basically exchanging life experiences. While I always think of a male transvestite as "he" in the United States, the Japanese transvestites' makeup was so perfect, and their mannerisms so distinctly feminine (unlike the transvestite in America who exaggerates gestures), that I shortly found myself thinking of them as "she." At the evening's onset, they all maintained complete satisfaction with their relationships with their families and with their way of life. As the night wore on, and the bottles of sake and beer accumulated, their previously contented façades paled, and they spoke ruefully of estrangement from their families, and alienation from the community. I found it incredibly sad. When my companion hypothetically offered them a pill that would produce heterosexuality, they all volunteered as potential purchasers, with the exception of the "actress," who really was enjoying his life. I cannot pass on the validity or "meaning" inherent in this experience. Were they just playacting, or conning the *gaijin* (outsider)? I doubt it. I was with one of their countrymen, and there was no financial gain for them. I felt something basic had been exposed, and that it extended far beyond the shores of their island.

How Does Homosexuality Happen to Happen: Etiology

Three approaches to the "why" of homosexuality are: (1) a normal variance; (2) born homosexual; and (3) a family affair. While there are no definitive conclusions, they all merit consideration, since they impact on the homosexual's sense of himself, and on society's attitudes toward the gay life.

A Normal Variance

The argument is made that homosexuality is merely a statistical departure from the norm. It is rife throughout the animal kingdom (giraffes do it, bonobo monkeys do it, and dolphins are occasionally known to do it) so why should our species be any different? A counter to this might be that, as far as we know, homosexuality in animals is more an occasional happenstance than a lifelong orientation. But, who knows? Therefore, it may be no more deviant than a red-headed individual in a predominantly brunette society, or a left-handed golfer in a shop filled with right-handed clubs. This stance was dramatically articulated when a group of thirty gay activists broke into a meeting of the American Psychiatric Association in the spring of 1971 and commandeered the podium. Their leader excoriated the two thousand psychiatrists in attendance in the audience with: "We are here to denounce your authority to call us 'sick' or mentally disordered . . ." He won the day when homosexuality was erased as a "mental disorder" by the APA two years later after a poll of all the members of the association.

Precisely what is meant by "sickness" or "disorder"? Is homosexuality an "illness" in the medical sense, à la schizophrenia, or is it rather a "difference" that our culture erroneously labels "sick" because it doesn't conform to accepted societal standards? Before any heterosexuals impetuously leap to any conclusions, they should ask themselves how they would function as heterosexuals in an exclusively homosexual culture, in which heterosexuality is a punishable offense. Those who would be symptom-free should be both applauded and wondered at. Since some homosexuals feel satisfied with their lives and appear as well adjusted or as equally neurotic as the average heterosexual, any connotation of "abnormality" on other than a statistical basis can be challenged. If, on the other hand, one assumes that heterosexuality is "obviously" the natural mode of development in all animal species since we seem to be programmed to procreate and expand our numbers, it follows that the homosexual has somehow been deflected from the normal developmental path. Furthermore, this "deviant" adaptation would still be aberrant regardless of the response of any particular society. The issue of our particular societal prejudice is of questionable validity in this context since, with the exception of ancient Greece and pre-Meiji Japan, homosexuality has been regarded as deviant in all but a few minor subcultures. Even the Greeks distinguished a socially sanctioned "pederasty," a love of boys, from the exclusively homosexual life, which was less esteemed. While the label of "deviancy" may be nothing more than a manifestation of historical ignorance, it may equally reflect the collective wisdom of generations. The lines seem drawn, but the question has only been resolved in minds already closed.

Born Homosexual

A tempting hypothesis is that homosexuality is the expression of some inherent biological abnormality, genetic or hormonal. The effeminate homosexual, the "queen," and the masculine-appearing lesbian, the "butch" or "dyke," make the onlooker wonder whether they are in some way physically or physiologically different from other members of their sex. The overwhelming majority of homosexuals of both sexes, however, cannot be distinguished as such by even the most sophisticated of observers, including other homosexuals, and, as previously mentioned, some cross-dressers are not homosexuals, while transsexuals, who are convinced that they are basically females imprisoned in male bodies, are dealing with problems unrelated to homosexuality.

Research excursions into a genetic basis for a homosexual adaptation have been intriguing, but, so far, inconclusive. Studies of twins have been the primary focus. A summation of their findings are: 57 percent of identical twins, 24 percent of nonidentical twins, and 13 percent of brothers of gay males are also gay, and that similar percentages are to be found within the lesbian population. While these figures may whet the appetites of those seeking the "gay gene," how does one explain the 43 percent of monozygotic twins who are not gay? Ergo, to date, the elusive gay gene either does not exist, is a meaningful factor only among some gay men, or influences sexual behavior in an as yet unknown fashion. Additionally, there may be other genetic factors still unidentified. For example, homosexuals tend to be born later in the sibling chain than would be expected on a statistical basis. They are more often the youngest, or near the youngest, of their brothers and sisters. While this might only reflect a close-binding relationship to a mother whose sexual relatedness with her husband had waned over the years, inducing her to seek emotional gratification from her "baby," it might be one more situation in which subtle chromosomal changes occur with aging parents that are then passed on to their offspring.

Animal studies, both pre- and postnatal, with injections of varied sex hormones at critical stages of development, have also been intriguing but inconclusive. Reports of abnormal breakdown products of testosterone and lower testosterone levels among homosexuals have been reported and discarded. It could not be determined whether the lower levels represented an etiologic factor, or, more likely, were the consequence of the gay lifestyle with its attendant stresses. It should be noted that attempts to "cure" homosexuality by the administration of testosterone only increased the person's sexual drive rather than altering its direction. It may prove to be the case that some prenatal hormonal event is a significant predisposing factor. Consider the possibility that there may be a difference in the quality or quantity of the male sex hormones during that portion of the life of the fetus during which the sexual responsivity centers of the brain are being "wired." Might this produce a tendency toward later responsivity to the same sex, while not interfering with the obvious anatomical development of the male? Dozens of hormonal theories have been promulgated in the past, at least as far back as 1892, only to be subsequently discarded. The response of the president of the Los Angeles Mattachine Society, Franklin Kameny, Ph.D., to these studies was that they were "no more relevant to the real problems of homosexuals than the biochemistry of melanin is to blacks." Enough said . . .

A Family Affair

The "Nature versus Nurture" controversy is a plague that has infested mankind with an "either-or" type of rational rigor mortis. Whether manifested in the educational field, race relations, childhood development, or homosexuality, the controversy encourages men to prematurely take rigid positions. Is homosexuality inherent in the individual's makeup, or are we dealing with a phenomenon engendered by environmental forces exacting their inexorable effects on the individual as he or she develops? The various biological approaches previously discussed generally fall under the "Nature" category. Theories of the experiential induction of homosexuality stresses the influence of environmental experiences, over and above, and possibly to the exclusion of, the "nature" one is born with. Clinicians are tempted to lean toward this position after becoming acquainted with life histories of their gay patients. When confronted with intimate data, especially details of family interrelationships, it is often difficult to see how an individual could have developed in any other direction. But then, there are always the exceptions . . .

The classic description of the family constellation most often associated with the etiology of male homosexuality was formulated by Irving Bieber and his associates in 1962, and has persisted to the present. Based on the premise that heterosexuality is the biological norm and that homosexuality is most probably the consequence of some environmental inhibition of normal heterosexual development, a postulation was made that specific family constellations might be ascertained that would most likely result in homosexuality. Close examination of the family backgrounds of 106 male homosexuals undergoing psychoanalytic treatment seemed to provide just such a constellation.

It was found that a family with a close-binding, overly intimate, and seductive mother, conjoined with a detached and hostile father, provided fertile soil for the development of homosexuality in a son. This typical mother dominates and demeans her husband, who often appears as a hostile intruder within the family. The destructive interaction between the parents is focused on a particular son, who then becomes the focus of the parents' pathology. Caught in a bind between his mother's closeness and seductiveness, and his father's hostility and distance, the boy must renounce his heterosexual strivings in his own self-defense. Identification and relationships with other men then become, in a sense, reparative, allowing for sexual expression, but in a fashion that reduces the threat inherent in heterosexual activities. Since sexual play with women is generally evocative of anxiety, there is a frequent fear of, and an aversion to, the female genitals. Heterosexual impotency may reflect a man's fear of real or symbolic castration as a punishment for his closeness to his mother, or her overpossessiveness may be so overwhelming that other women inspire the "vagina dentata" fantasy (the vagina with teeth), in which a man imagines the loss of his penis in a toothed vagina.

In most circumstances, the boy is attached to a mother who infantilizes him and discourages a free assertion and development of his masculinity, while, at the same time, he is deprived of an adequate father figure to identify with. An involved and loving father is rarer than a dinosaur egg in the families of gay men. As a boy matures, he finds himself cut off from a supportive and encouraging group of peers. Feeling himself an outsider, a loner, and a "queer," he naturally gravitates to others on the periphery, if they are available. Sooner or later, contact is made with someone more homosexually committed and a tentative resolution to his conflicts is found. Once he is introduced into the "gay scene," a more stable and accepting environment is available and his homosexual adaptation becomes further entrenched.

A further reinforcement for the environmental etiology of homosexuality was a similar investigation in 1967 of twenty-four female homosexuals undergoing psychoanalysis, in which I was the principal investigator. Again, a fairly typical family constellation emerged, in which the father appeared to play the stellar role. A composite picture of this father portrayed a man who appeared puritanical, yet manifested a seductive attitude toward his frightened daughter only slightly below the surface. He was overly possessive, attempting to exclude the mother, as well as friends, both male and female, from intimacy with his daughter. Excessively interested in her physical development, he simultaneously frowned upon her play with dolls, use of cosmetics, and other aspects of her female identification. In short, he discouraged her emergence as a functioning female. The image of a close-binding, overly intimate father mirrored the close-binding intimate mother found in the studies of male homosexuality.

An addendum to the above: with additional years of reflection and clinical experience, I am less convinced of the universal applicability of these studies, even though they have been replicated by other groups. While the research methodology and statistics still suffice, even allowing for the relatively restricted population studied, I have treated too many men and women, having the families just described, who are distinctly heterosexual. To further complicate matters, the chicken-and-the-egg argument obtrudes. For example, was the detached and hostile father this way from the beginning, or was this instead his reaction to a son who he was finding increasingly different and disappointing? Was the absence of play with dolls and cosmetics among the girls dictated by her father, or was it more a manifestation of the type of play seen among girls whose mothers received steroids during their pregnancies?

A somewhat different family constellation was ascertained in a later study of twenty-five homosexual girls in the New York City public school system, girls primarily from the lower socioeconomic group. The fathers of this group were characterized as "hostile, exploitative, detached, and absent," while the mothers appeared overburdened and unable to deal with their family responsibilities. These mothers often conveyed negative attitudes toward men to their daughters.

Family attitudes make their contribution to homosexual development; the question is, to what extent? Perhaps there is a spectrum, from "Nature" on one end, to "Nurture" on the other. It may be that those born with a weighted "Nature," require little push from the "Nurture" end, and vice versa.

Facts and Fictions

Legend has it that when the oracle at Delphi was asked if there was any man in Athens wiser than Socrates, the answer was "No one." Socrates, learning of this, ascribed it to his awareness of his own ignorance. On the topic of homosexuality, it is rare to find a Socrates these days.

Despite the paucity of data on homosexuality—etiology; pathology, if any; psychology, normal or abnormal; the visceral component of the varied lifestyles; the issues of morality; the "threat" they purportedly pose to our way of life and even to our civilization; and so forth—religious and political leaders, media personalities, and the more extreme homophobes of our citizenry pontificate as if they were blessed with deific knowledge. In their anti-Socratic posturing, they exhibit what can charitably be called hypocrisy, delusions, or their being intellectually disadvantaged, doing much harm in the process. Pat Robertson and Jerry Falwell are too absurd to be taken seriously with their hellfire-and-brimstone routines, but unfortunately, they are, by too many. Trent Lott, Senate majority leader, arch defender of campaign finance pandering, dares to compare homosexuals to kleptomaniacs. A "Dr." Laura Schlessinger, the self-designated "America's Moral Authority," who boasts of twenty million listeners to her radio talk show, is quoted by the *New York Times* as ranting: "Rights? For sexual deviants, sexual behavior, there are now rights? That's what I'm worried about with the pedophilia and the bestiality and the sadomasochism and the cross-dressing. Is this all going to be rights too? Why does deviant sexual behavior get rights?" And she introduces herself as "I am my kid's mom." The average straight guy has nothing to fear from the average gay guy. In the unlikely event that a feeble pass is thrown in his direction, he is by no means obliged to catch it. It is more likely to be a tribute to his attractiveness, rather than a threat to his masculinity. It has been observed that if a woman reacted in an eruptive fashion every time an unwanted pass was made at her, the human race would have died out ages ago. Obviously, one can go on and on. But beneath the bombast and the buffoonery there are real issues to be considered, some of which have a life-and-death significance.

Homosexuality is certainly more than simply a statistical deviation from the norm. The "abnormality" exposes some of the mysteries within which we enshroud sexuality, it runs counter to the evolutionary imperative to further promulgate the species, and, in its departure from the stereotype, it discombobulates the fragile masculine identities of so many fragile males. But the "abnormality" itself, in the collective judgment of mental health professionals, the psychiatrists and psychologists who actively deal with homosexuals on an everyday basis, is not an 'illness" in any sense of that term, nor is it deemed to be an entity that warrants "treatment" or "change." We "treat" both homosexual and heterosexual people who have problems, but very few therapists envision changing someone's sexual orientation as "the" purpose of therapy, or as an end in itself. There are some homosexuals, probably within Kinsey's grade 3 or 4, who have altered their orientation, but I am aware of no one within the grade 6 range (exclusively homosexual in fantasy, dreams, and activities) who has made the transition to heterosexuality, and, consequently, they should not be pushed into therapy to effectuate a reorientation. On the other hand, those wavering in a homo-heterosexual limbo, in Kinsey's 3, 4, or possibly 5 area, who are sufficiently dissatisfied with the gay life, might make an attempt to change via therapy. If a successful transition to heterosexuality is accomplished, fine; if, on the other hand, this is impractical, then aiming for a successful easement into a homosexual adaptation would seem a reasonable objective. There have been unfortunate situations where homosexual behavior was made so taboo that sexual activities were totally suppressed, to the detriment of the person.

The public must understand that people do not "choose" to be homosexual, that it is instead an orientation they develop from their earliest years. Some gay men, unfortunately known as "sissy boys," shunned the typically boyish rough-and-tumble play, and preferred to play with girls and dolls, from the cradle onward, surely not a consciously directed election. The transvestite does not "choose" to become aroused by wearing feminine clothing, he feels compelled to do so. The transsexual male feels that he is a female trapped in a male body; again, no question of a choice. In fact, given the persecutions, and the trials and tribulations inherent in the gay life today, if any adult consciously chose to be gay, one would assume the presence of a significant psychiatric problem until proven otherwise.

If a witch hunt for psychopathology is to be conducted within the homosexual arena, it is far more likely to be found among homophobic and antigay groups. Why should their detestation, hatred, and even violence be so virulent? What cataclysms have homosexuals inflicted on humanity? Schlessinger's pratings about pedophilia and sadomasochism apply equally to heterosexuals, or has the good "doctor" never heard of female dominatrices? Yet Bill Clinton all but destabilized the United States via his heterosexuality, and the actual destroyers of civilizations, Mao, Stalin, Hitler, Milosevic, Saddam Hussein, et al., have all been heterosexual, but antiheterosexual vendettas are not even dreamed of. Gay bashers, on the other hand, seem strangely insensitive to the contributions homosexuals have made to civilization, and unwilling to credit the contributions made by the hordes of homosexuals who have enriched the fabric of our culture, from Leonardo to Sondheim.

The roots of their hatred sink dark and deep into the nether regions where one finds anti-Semitism, racism, blood feuds, and the like. Religions have been in the vanguard, with burnings, torture, and other unpleasantness, in the church's authoritarian attempts to control their flocks by strictly limiting their access to pleasure (see chapter 4). Piously invoking the authority of Scripture, religious leaders vehemently proclaim the homosexual a sinner, although Christ never mentioned the subject, nor was it addressed in the Gospels. There are only two references to it in the Old Testament (in Leviticus), and it is passingly dealt with in the New Testament, primarily by Saint Paul (see Romans 1:26–27). Christ's admonitions against the accumulation of wealth and his plea for the brotherhood of man are conveniently ignored. Ergo, this animosity extends deeper than mere Scripture.

Descending to a darker level, one meets the concept of "the Other," in which one cultural group coheres together, and perceives the extruded group as "evil," and as the externalized personification of their internal hatreds, conflicts, and insecurities. For example, while gay bashers justify their bashing by blaming the sexual license and "deviant"

sexual practices in the gay community, they might themselves dream or fantasize about oral and anal intercourse and
other licentious delectations that they would never admit to
themselves or their wives. When these desires are more consciously recognized, they hate themselves for having them.
Better to bash a gay guy. A similar process occurs in anti-
Semitism and racism. To the medieval Catholics, the image
of the Jew may easily be a projection of their disappointments with their own religion (if God is good, who is to
blame for the evils that have befallen me? Guess who!), insecurities about their own faith with a consequent circling-
the-wagons mentality, the rottenness they feel about
themselves (as personified by the "dirty Jew"), and the perceived failure of a presumably benevolent universe to bestow
any kindnesses upon them. And to the Caucasian, the black
has the superior strength, the larger penis, a feral masculinity
that can easily overwhelm a white woman, and a better jump
shot to boot. "The Other" is more overtly seen in the current
blood feuds between the Hutus and the Tutsis in Rwanda,
and the Serbs and the Albanians in Kosovo.

Apparently, antigay bias is much more than a casual
glitch in the social screen.

Truth and Consequences

Problems inherent in the homosexual dilemma lie less
within the individual homosexual, and evidently become
more the problem of society. The rifts in the social fabric
referential to homosexuality—gay marriage (which will be

touched upon in the final chapter), gay rights, gays in the military, gay curricula in schools and so on—generally fall within the purview of the politicians and various social scientists.

However, society's negative impacts on the individual homosexual are easily recognized. The devaluation and abuse heaped upon the individual gay by his environment and his family, the resultant sense of devaluation, the blows to his self-esteem, isolation from his peers, and finally physical abuse, are common knowledge. Both casual and committed homophobes may be insufficiently aware of the depth and sharpness of the damage they inflict on their fellow humans. As an example, consider the incidence of suicide in gay youths.

The U.S. Government's report of a task force on youth suicide, published in 1989, indicated that "gay youths were 2 to 3 times more likely to attempt suicide than non-gays, and that they may comprise up to 30 percent of completed youth suicides annually." Dr. Gary Remafedi's summation of other studies, published in the October 6, 1999, issue of the *Journal of the American Medical Association*, indicated that while these suicides were not attributable to homosexuality per se, "they were significantly associated with gender non-conformity, early awareness of homosexuality, stress, violence, lack of support, school drop-out, family problems, acquaintances' suicide attempts," and others. Similar studies in Canada, Minnesota, and Massachusetts found similar associations. And this is just one of the many sins visited upon men who happen to be gay.

In summary, homosexuals are neither angels nor devils, but rather are people, with their own uniqueness, who constitute an integral part of the social landscape. Their participation in society, and the attitudes of the environment that surrounds them, should be directed at understanding and conciliation. To those either casually or vehemently antigay, remember that homophobia can be lethal. Human beings are destroyed or die; there are consequences.

7

The Crunch

Inevitably, the phantasm of the Masculine Mystique collides with the actualities of the average man's existence. The irresistible fantasy confronts the immovable reality and, with the collision of the juggernauts, the male finds himself caught in the Crunch, squeezed between the jaws of a cosmic vise.

The Mystique, extolling a heroic independence, a sequence of courageous confrontations met by achievement and exploits, has shown no evidence of relaxing its imperatives. Theodore Roosevelt's "man in the arena" thesis may serve as a prototype. Roosevelt exhorted: "The credit belongs to the man who is actually in the arena, whose face is marred with sweat and dust and blood; who errs and comes short again and again; who knows the great enthusiasms, the great devotions, and spends himself in a worthy cause; who, if he wins, knows the triumph of high achievement; and who, if he fails, at least fails while daring greatly, so that his place shall never be with those cold and timid souls who know neither victory nor defeat." If you have blood, how can it fail to be stirred! Following this thesis, man's life is a never-ending gladiatorial contest on the sun-drenched sands of a contemporary coliseum. Lest it be dismissed as some prehistoric relic of those derring-do days of the early twentieth century, it should be noted that these words have been admiringly invoked by President Kennedy and identified with by most present-day politicians during their more testicular displays.

The opposing jaw of the vise, the more prosaic and frequently piddling actualities of a man's day-to-day experience appear pallid by contrast. With the rare exception of the beneficently blessed Internet zillionaires most men, after all, strive to climb a few more rungs on a seemingly limitless ladder. High achievement is highly uncommon, a statistical fluke that few attain or even have access to. Perhaps heroism consists, in part, of defying the odds; but we all know those who have successfully surmounted them. Even in the most honest of lotteries and casinos, the few walk away with the winnings, while the multitude eventually acquiesce to the probabilities. In striving to attain the seductive realm of the Mystique, while skidding on the slippery shoals of his own uncertain world, a man's reach may well exceed his grasp. He hazards a fall, and an unflattering blow to his ego.

In place of Henley's challenge to the winds, "I am the master of my fate; I am the captain of my soul," a more insightful man might say, "My mastery is limited by my male biology; by the circumstances of my birth; by the hands I am dealt by chance; by the constraints of my society; and by a lack of awareness about myself, of my limitations and my potentials. But, if knowledge is power, let me grasp all the knowledge of myself that I can."

Limitations and Liabilities: Songs Your Mother Never Sang To You

From an actuarial standpoint, maleness itself must be considered somewhat of a handicap, for men comprise the more vulnerable half of the species. If a male fetus, nestled in the quietude of the womb, was cognizant and capable of contemplating his future, he might develop survival anxiety early in the game. Since life seems to consist of one series of probabilities after another, he would be bound to be dismayed and appalled by the statistical disadvantages suffered by men, when compared with women.

Even in the sanctuary of the uterus, more males than females die before birth, and 25 percent more boys are born prematurely, and with more congenital defects than girls. The cleft lips and strictures of the esophagus and rectum are more common in male babies.

At the moment of birth, the male neonate's life expectancy is six years less than his female counterpart, who will likely survive 79.1 years to his 73.1. Inequity plagues the newborn male immediately after surviving the discomfitures of birth. Even during the first year of life, he runs a

10 percent greater mortality risk, is more prone to a crib death, and even though male fetuses tend to tarry in the womb a few extra days, a baby girl's respiratory and circulatory systems are likely to be in better shape. Three to four times as many boys are born autistic, and twice as many boys are born with a club foot. Baby boys cry more, sleep less, and are more active and demanding. Girls smile more, with more to smile about.

In the nursery and through their early school years, hyperactivity syndromes are 95 percent more likely to be found in males, as is dyslexia (400 percent), which may partially account for the increased learning disabilities that plague the boy student.

Assuming that the fledgling male survives these early hazards, what might he look forward to? Men are at a far higher risk of leaving this vale of tears through suicide or homicide than women. In 1997, the ratio of victims of violent crimes was 45.8 male to 33.0 female. On the medical front, men are more prone to leukemia, and cancer of the skin, larynx, bladder, kidney, stomach, central nervous system, lymphatic system, and lungs. While women might point to cancer of the breast, men can easily counter with cancer of the prostate, with both being approximately equally deadly. The American Cancer Society's projection for the year 2000 foresaw 40,800 deaths from breast cancer, and 31,900 fatalities from cancer of the prostate. But consider, as an additional factor, that the male runs a 1 in 6 probability of developing prostatic malignancy, while a woman's odds of breast cancer are 1 in 9. Flip a coin. Yet funds devoted to research into these diseases are not remotely equal; far more moneys are allocated to breast research, with the prostate still in the role of the stepchild. When women complain of the interminable lines for the ladies' room at the theater, while the men seem to breeze in and out of the gents' room, they might consider it a small trade-off paid for their extended life spans. To add a few psychiatric fillips, the male is three times more vulnerable to obsessive-compulsive disorders, five to ten times more prone to become a sociopathic personality, and, as far as sexual deviations are concerned, I suggest a remembrance of chapter 4, "The Sex Life of a Penis." How many female exhibitionists or voyeurs does the average pedestrian encounter?

The myth that all men are created equal is a fanciful, well-intentioned fairy tale, i.e., they are obviously born with different levels of genetic potential, which call for neither shame nor apology. This is simply a fact of life. Ditto for the discrepancy between men and women. Biologically, women emerge with survivorship nestled between their bosoms. Yet the Mystique, having little stomach for statistics, urges the male to flex his biological resources, to strain his not unlimited capacities, to emulate the Neanderthal Ideal, and to finally collapse from the Crunch.

In its obsession with performance and achievement, the Mystique is seemingly oblivious to the circumstances surrounding each individual's birth and development. In their self-assessments, men rarely take these Mystique-discounted contingencies into account. But, as W. C. Fields snortingly advised: "Let's grab the bull by the tail and face the situation."

The male fetus greets the world as a tiny, helpless, illiterate, and barely formed hunk of protoplasm. His inheritance, his genetic makeup, is already fixed, and at this stage of medical progress he can't do a thing to change it. The family he enters is also an established entity. It will be incumbent upon them to nurture, protect, socialize, and educate him. But who are "they" and what are "they" like? Where do they stand socially and economically? Infant mortality, for example, is 50 to 100 percent higher if one's parents are in the lowest socioeconomic segment. If his mother is a teenaged kid herself, what nurturing and socialization can she supply? What is the family's attitude toward the newcomer? Was he wanted; were they selecting girls' names instead of boys'; and what is their approach to child rearing? Is the father an adequate male to identify with, an upbeat, encouraging figure, or is he one of those passive and distant fellows? Will the mother be overprotective or domineering? If she is indulgent and lacks discipline, her son may turn out infantile, demanding, and always expecting instant gratification. On the other hand, neurosis, submission, anxiety, and excessive inhibitions may menacingly loom if she is overly domineering. Caring, nurturing mothers have a predilection for infecting their children with a precious optimism. Where does one draw the line? How will these constellations affect his "valiant striving" or his "great enthusiasms"?

To further complicate matters, the fetus is born with his own spark of the divine fire, a temperament of his own. If his parents are quiet souls, how will they react to a robust and tumultuous son? On the other hand, if the boy happens to enjoy a certain contemplative serenity, will he be a comfort or a disappointment to an action-oriented couple? If the characteristics of parents and child coincide, the infant is truly blessed. The possibilities and permutations are staggering enough, but the boy must somehow muddle through them, saddled with the Mystique.

While parents exert their appropriate and time-honored influence upon their child, the birth order of the boy has its own influences and inducements to weave into his psychic tapestry. If the newborn happens to be the first-born, his chances of achievement and eminence soar. The majority of listings in *Who's Who*, the bulk of American scientists, and most of the Rhodes Scholars have tradition-ally been the first child or only children. Apparently, the firstborn gets an initial boost up the ladder. But most boosts have some backlash. Alfred Adler referred to firstborns as "power-hungry conservatives," and a craving for predom-inance thrusts the child directly into the path of the Mys-tique's Dominance Drive. Since the first child has a stake in preserving the status quo, he tends to be morally and politically more conservative than his rebellious younger siblings. When Gilbert and Sullivan wrote that every man alive was born a liberal or a conservative, they were not far from the mark. How much choice, or "free will," does the growing male really have? Isn't the freedom of decision and action inherent in the Mystique's Heroic Imperative? The firstborn is apt to have a more highly developed conscience, to be more curious and cooperative, and to be found vol-unteering for psychological experimentation. He is also a prime candidate for enlistment in the service of the Mys-tique.

If the newborn has one or more predecessors, his life-style might be significantly different. Youngest children are the family "babies," tend to remain so, and are magnets for more than their fair share of attention. They consequently are prone to become actors, constantly amassing applause and recognition in their lifelong quest to monopolize the limelight. A study of leading comedians (the criteria being years in the business, income, et cetera) found a cookie-cutter similarity. They were overwhelmingly youngest children, very closely attached to their mothers, and were extremely fond of children.

In the unhappy event that the fetus emerges as a middle child, he might reconsider and remain in the unpressured womb indefinitely. Pushed down by their seniors and constantly challenged by their juniors, the middles feel a sardinelike psychic squash. Special tribute should be paid to successful middle children; they've made it against the odds, and with no discernible positional advantage working for them.

Other preexisting determinants envelop the newborn, waiting to shape his future personality and to influence his attainments. Consider his family's socioeconomic status as an example, going beyond the obvious differences in social and material advantages that define affluence and poverty. A boy born to the upper class, who has therefore a lessened likelihood of homicide, psychosis, or suicide, has a 400 percent greater chance of being referred for psychiatric help by his family physician should psychological problems arise. A boy entering a middle-class milieu is a potential prey to the Achiever complex, to be caught in the bind between the surge for upward mobility, skyward to the upper economic realms, versus the improbability of making it. Or dwell upon the psychology of the socioeconomically deprived youngster. Facing economic hardship and a much higher probability of a broken home, brittle relationships, and an absentee father, the boy finds that the mere struggle for existence becomes a major preoccupation, and the nuances of psychological development may become negligible or coarsened in the process. Growing up deprived may often be associated with poor impulse control. Since the capacity to internalize one's impulses is a prerequisite for progressing, handicaps mount. Fragmented families frequently germinate rage-filled children; and rage plus poor impulse control equals confrontation with the law. A sorry case, calling for any bright innovations that a boy's nimble brain can devise. Obviously, many succeed, and their accomplishments and associated stratagems should be more widely disseminated. But the boy's brain will not be working for his best advantage. Thus, as a member of the impoverished, he is more likely to have a visual rather than an aural orientation, which would present problems in classroom lectures and in following verbal instructions; to develop an external stance rather than becoming introspective, which might diminish his creativity; to center around content rather than form, allowing him to lose the forest for the trees; to become problem-centered rather than being comfortable with abstract thinking (a wayfarer in our complex society is at a loss without a developed capacity for abstract thought); to develop a spatial rather than a temporal conceptualization, making the concept of time relatively less important; and to be more expressive than instrumental, allowing for the perception of misery, but lacking the wherewithal to do much about it. He thus develops with an orientation precisely opposite to that required to improve his inherited lot.

On the more biochemical level, the tyranny of the testicles has gained increased recognition and appreciation as a potent "given," a controlling factor in the male psyche. With testosterone washing every cell in the male's body, he becomes subtly more impelled to adopt a risk-taking orientation, to become more confrontational and aggressive, and to exert less control when urges emerge. It primes him, not only for battle, but for assertion. Compare the randy seventeen-year-old boy making a premature pass at a female classmate to that enchanting roué Maurice Chevalier, at seventy-two, explaining to Alan Jay Lerner that he was now comfortable with being too old for women (resulting in Lerner's writing the lyric for the song in *Gigi* entitled "I'm Glad I'm Not Young Anymore," which Chevalier sang with such élan). A difference in testosterone levels? It is theorized that the more testicularly dominated may opt for careers involving more risk-taking and aggression, from Tony Soprano, trial lawyers, and professional athletes on the one hand, to the Oxford don and the contract lawyer on the other. Additionally, due to an increased urge to explore, men are more prone to extramarital affairs and their consequent sexually transmitted diseases. How the genetic, biochemical, and environmental do seem to intertwine. To what extent is the average chap aware of this, and what can he do about it?

On a brighter note: although the doctrine of predestination is lately out of style, it is evident that men are born with more rigidities and limitations than the Mystique would admit to. It is equally evident that some men create greater latitudes and options for themselves than do their peers. The "givens" in a man's life are not absolutes, but rather define the likely scope, framework, and patterns of response that he brings into each unique or challenging experience. Patterns can be modified and obstacles overcome by dint of intelligence, effort, motivation, and perseverance, but only a rare soul (if he exists at all) can totally divest himself of his "givens" and conform to that pure masculine essence envisioned by the Mystique. I would suggest that a man think of himself as a "player," a gamesman who can survey his field, know his options, and play with an animated involvement that gives him a feeling of "fun." Any gambler should know the odds, even those of filling an inside straight. Socrates said that the unexamined life is not worth living. Well, that's putting it a bit strong, but the examined life is better lived, and the examination of the "givens" of one's life, contrasted with the absurdities of the Mystique, might soften the Crunch, and allow for some stimulating creativity.

A Woman Is a Sometime Thing

The women's movement has recently loomed as a more potent contributor to the Crunch, impacting the male in virtually every area of his life. In the first scene of Gershwin's opera *Porgy and Bess,* Clara sings the hauntingly beautiful lullaby "Summertime" to her baby, while a crap game is being played downstage. Her husband, Jake, breaks away from the game to actually sing the child to sleep with his more sapient "A Woman Is a Sometime Thing," in which "woman may born you, love you an' mourn you," but she still remains a "sometime thing." With the rise of the women's movement (WM), women have indeed become more "sometime" to the average guy. From onetime singers of lullabies, women have become increasingly discontent with playing second fiddle in the masculine symphony, and are demanding at least equal time on the podium. More pointedly, the traditional assumption of male supremacy and dominance is being challenged and threatened for the first time in history. The twenty-first century may well be recorded as the Century of the Woman. Since it impacts all areas of men's lives (academia, work, military, sex, and divorce courts to name but a few), attention must indeed be paid.

Recall the Yang-Yin construct described in chapter 2, with the male principle, Yang, embodying the positive, while Yin, the female principle, exemplified all that is negative. While men have been comforted by this for the last three thousand years, the WM now abruptly announces that this is simply and unutterably wrong, and that a wholesale reassessment is called for. More basso than lyric soprano, no lullaby here! Let's play. How about these positions for openers:

Basic to male-female interactions is not an unalterable set of divine decrees, but is, instead, a power transaction in which the male has accrued all the trump cards, and will not part willingly with any of his prerogatives. Be it in the workplace, the family, or academia, expect no largesse from men.

The preservation of male power necessitates the dehumanization of women and the stultification of their individualities. The oppressive subjugation of women has not simply occurred by happenstance, but reflects some grand patriarchal scheme, which allows men to retain their pre-eminent position. This hypothesis assumes a tacit conspiracy, consensually agreed upon, not only by males inhabiting this planet at this particular time, but by all males who have lived through the previous millennia. The violence, abuse, and harassment that women endure are the inevitable consequences of this cabal.

The family structure, as presently constituted, may be passé and dysfunctional. It is ill-suited to the explosive numbers of illegitimate children, it entraps women in a condition of quasi-servitude, and is often an ineffective child-rearing institution that visits the psychopathology of the parents upon their offspring.

Boys and girls are born with few, if any, differentiating features other than their reproductive apparatus. While a nod should be given to a few physiological and hormonal factors, nurture easily takes precedence over nature. The differences one discerns in temperament and social roles are primarily due to "socialization" or "brainwashing" perpetuated by a culture that imprints its distorted concepts of masculinity and femininity on impressionable and previously unstructured minds. This thesis has a philosophical kinship with that of John Locke, the apostle of the Revolution of 1688. In his famed exposition of the tabula rasa, Locke says: "Let us suppose the mind to be, as we say, white paper, void of all characters, without any ideas; how comes it to be furnished?" A segment of the feminist community has had its rather definitive answer, at least in the male-female category.

Society's intrusion into women's bodies is bizarre and

appalling. Consider how threatening a woman's body must be perceived in Orthodox Jewish and Muslim and other fundamentalist communities, in which men must be protected against, and artificially separated from, even normal nonsexual contact with women. Why? Enough of this nonsense! A woman's body belongs to her and to her alone. It is not the business of society or the patriarchs who run it to dictate whether she can empty her own uterus, be a lesbian or a prostitute, or wear rings in her navel, nipples, or nostrils. And by the way, my male Republican chums, how dare you try to screw around with *Roe* v. *Wade!*

Since women are at least equal to men, they should enjoy the same opportunities as do their male brethren in all areas. The vocational, educational, business, political, military, and athletic venues should all be fair game for the fair sex. And, to push it a wee bit, considering the millennia of deprivation, how about a little preferential treatment? Let's raise the ante.

The majority of women are still either not aware of, nor are they sufficiently attuned to, their oppressed state. Ergo, their consciousness must be raised, and there should be armies of their sisters to assist them in achieving their fundamental rights.

And these are just openers. More hands remain to be dealt.

An initial survey of the gender war zone can resemble debris scattered across the social landscape. The WM has certainly wreaked its share of havoc, so much of which is understandable and justified. While not discounting other volcanic upsurgences (economic, technological upheavals, medical miracles, and the like), the WM is surely a major player, and is only ignored at the peril of not noticing a mastodon in your living room.

As discussed in chapter 5, the patriarchal predicate of the family has been severely dented. Illegitimate births, one-third of all births, have become so prevalent that DNA testing for paternity is beginning to outweigh family structure as a determinant of paternity.

On the vocational front, the widely heralded "glass ceiling" is rapidly shattering. In the summer of 1999, a forty-four-year-old woman, Ms. Carleton Fiorina, was named chief executive of Hewlett-Packard, the first woman to head a Fortune 100 company, while Colonel Eileen McCollins became the first woman to command a space shuttle. Whatever happened to the simple joys of maidenhood?

Simultaneously, median wages for men had fallen, while those of women were on the rise, and the percentage of women with jobs had risen to 55 percent. The growth rate of jobs for women exceeded that for men. The premium on brawn, either explicitly or implicitly exercised, has rapidly declined, with women replacing the muscular with the cerebral. Additionally, let us not overlook the feminist demands for equal or preferential treatment echoing down the corridors of the human resources divisions of every major corporation. There are no similar exhortations to be heard from the male sex.

The ivied walls of academia have acquired an increasingly feminine tint. Fifty-five percent of college students are women, and the majority of applicants and acceptees to graduate schools such as medicine are also female. Zealous demands by zealous feminists have altered the tone of academic discourse, forcibly replacing writings of venerable white males with somewhat less than venerable works by women writers of all colors. Women's programs are now a part of the standard academic establishment, while similar much needed male programs have yet to reach the state of never-never land. Judicially sanctioned all-female schools flourish in the same atmosphere that holds all-male schools to be taboo. Issues of "political correctness," as well as sexual harassment, may have had the effect of putting the blessings of wide-ranging give-and-take intellectual discourse into a straitjacket, but some women see this as a small price to pay to advance their agenda. Lopsidedly, while female journalists have been granted a legal imprimatur to invade male locker rooms to interview the male bodies therein, and do, I am not aware of men being accorded similar access to women's locker rooms, and availing themselves of the opportunity.

The massive entry of women into the military has become an obvious and widely discussed fact of life, as has their significant rates of pregnancies and consequent discharge. Whether their performance, and their request for equality in assignment, promotion, and responsibility puts men in harm's way remains to be seen. Will this eventually be happily resolved, or will the esprit de corps become dispirited and diminished?

Even the vagina has come out of the closet. Consciousness-raising groups have made women more aware of, and more comfortable with, their sexual and reproductive apparatus. This is happily proclaimed in the current stage hit *The Vagina Monologues*, in which a group of actresses of the stature of Glenn Close, Whoopi Goldberg, and Winona Ryder have appeared in various productions, dressed in red velvet, to entertainingly discuss the female sexual apparatus and appetites to sophisticated and hip audiences. So much for the myth of male sexual superiority! And this is just the tip of the proverbial iceberg.

Some Consequences

Having lived with the Mystique all their lives, men barely notice the Crunch, somewhat like primitives chronically infested with parasites, who accept weakness and debilitation as a "natural" part of their lives. "If we knew, all the gods would awake," wrote Guillaume Apollinaire; but few are aware, and the gods continue their sleep. Perhaps it's about time they got off their couches. The symptoms of the Crunch are so pandemic, and men have become so habituated to them, that they are rarely recognized until the squeeze begins to pinch and the hurt is registered. The ache may appear in the physical, psychological, or psychosomatic spheres, but since men have been programmed to respond only to the obvious and painful wound ("little boys don't cry," and brave men barely wince), a relatively painless malignancy is allowed to develop. Some remedies will be suggested in the next chapter.

Consequential to his service as the family emissary to the outer world, the male most directly confronts change, economic upheaval, social pressure, and similar stresses. Even in a family with shared responsibilities, it is usually the man who must bear that ultimate and final survival responsibility, the last stop in the passage of the buck. It is frequently the unremitting pressure, the unending insecurity, or the unrelenting monotony that produces the steady influx of stress that eventually exhausts whatever coping mechanisms many men possess.

There is little doubt that the stress of daily living wreaks its toll of coronaries upon the hearts of men. The death rate from coronary artery disease among white men aged thirty-five to forty-four is 6.1 times that among age-matched white women. Estrogen protects the premenopausal woman, but does stress condemn the man? An elevation of the blood level of cholesterol has long been recognized as a major factor in increasing the probability of a coronary. When the cholesterol levels of group of accountants were monitored during a year, their cholesterol was observed to steeply rise from mid-March through mid-April, corresponding to the stress of the tax season. Corporate accountants, whose deadlines occur at the year's end, showed no springtime elevation. It is rather unlikely that this relationship between work stress and elevated cholesterol levels is confined to the accounting profession. A presumptive coronary-prone behavior pattern, the type A personality, had been delineated. Characterized by intense striving for achievement, competitiveness, aggressivity, impatience, a preemptive speech pattern, and a constant awareness of the pressure of time and responsibility, the male candidate for a coronary is a living embodiment of the ideals of the Mystique.

While peptic ulcer is considered primarily an illness associated with the bacteria *H. pylori,* the contributory effects of stress cannot be discounted. Germaine Greer, commenting on women entering into the commercial arena (male territory), welcomed them "to the world of the ulcer and the coronary."

Air traffic controllers added an additional dimension to the man-stress-ulcer syndrome. At one time, more than 85 percent of air traffic controllers, under the constant stress of making instantaneous life-and-death decisions, showed clinical symptoms of peptic ulcers, while 32.5 percent evidenced that ulcerous niche on barium X rays. An extreme example? Of course. Does it have applicability to other men? Probably.

The riddles of hypertension (high blood pressure) are still to be solved. Its causation, multifaceted, likely includes the stress factor. Consider this relationship between anger and hypertension. Pairs of college students had their fingers attached to electric shocking devices, which allowed one to give a shock to the other. The subjects who received a series of shocks evidenced a rise in their blood pressures. If the shockee could then shock his shocker in return, his blood pressure fell. If this retaliation was prevented, his blood pressure remained elevated for a longer period of time. How many men, with their livelihoods, families, or careers at stake, have to sit by and "take it," without having the means or the capacity to respond or to rectify a grievance? What effect does it have on their arteries?

Moving from the psychosomatic to the psychic, suicide, the ninth major cause of death in the United States, emerges as an additional male prerogative. Men kill themselves five times as often as do women, although the latter make more attempts (in 1996, 24,998 men, while only 5,905 women suicided). Either men are more skilled in killing themselves, or they have more to kill themselves about.

These are but a few of the more egregious expressions of the Crunch. The drive for achievement found among sufferers of gout (although gout has an unquestionably organic causation), or the diminution of testosterone production in men under stress, might also be mentioned, along with dozens of illustrations embedded in the preceding chapters on work, sex, and marriage. Each man, on reflection, can add his own syndromes to what appears to be an interminable list.

The Crunch is the consequence of the Mystique's misperception of the male as a creature of infinite potentials and inexhaustible capacities. Since men, as a group, have not attained this deific stature, but the individual man is blessed with his own individuality and talents, a unique blend of the superb and the limited, a sense of rational perspective is required for a semblance of satisfactory survival. As to that matter of a satisfactory survival, I suggest turning the page to that final chapter.

8

That Matter of Survival

A Zen parable portrays a man hanging halfway down the side of a steep escarpment, desperately clinging to a slim vine. On the ground below, a tigress and her hungry cubs await his arrival, salivating with anticipation. Above, two mice busily gnaw away at the root stalk of his lifeline. An awkward situation. He spies a black orchid blossoming from the cliff wall, a hypnotic palette of iridescent pastels. "How beautiful," he murmurs.

And so this cursory sketch of the average male's existential landscape, with its various absurdities and trepidations, inevitably ends with a portrait of an embattled and endangered species deserving of strenuous efforts at study and conservation. Manipulated by the Mystique, squeezed in the Crunch, the male requires more than token assistance to maintain even a modicum of humane function. In fact, the time may be ripe to achieve an overall enhancement of the quality of his life. A civilized survival, in the physical, psychological, and social senses of that primordial term, demands individual and collective ingenuity to devise, learn, and adapt to changed ground rules. Today's man has but one lone lifetime at his disposal. We must help the poor fellow get off that vine as expeditiously as possible; the blandishments of the orchid will no longer suffice.

Obviously, the male will continue to be buffeted by forces beyond his control: geopolitical, macroeconomic, and the like. The role of pure chance, so often underappreciated, must be factored in as well. Some of the elements more within his control have been the subject of this book the Mystique, the vagaries of the masculine role, his relationship with women, and what the future might hold for him. Ergo, a summation and some emphasis.

During the murky mists of time while the male was evolving into today's man, the Masculine Mystique evolved with him, as another coping device to allow him to better survive in his environment. The Neanderthal Ideal encouraged the brawn essential for existence in a hostile environment, the Heroic Imperative allowed him to lead the charge with grace, the Sexual Athlete increased his progeny, the Dominance Drive and Achiever Complex expanded his domain and provided him with the illusion of mastery, while the Playboy image added a necessary dollop of fun to keep things going. And it worked; until now. Radical changes have been shaking society's substructure within the past several decades, with evolutionary reformulations of gender roles constantly taking place. But like an authoritarian regime imploding from internal inconsistencies, mismanagement, and just being passed by as antiquated, the Mystique has pathetically overplayed its role, and refused to adapt. It should have the decency to retire from the scene, or be forcibly ousted, as the now dysfunctional device it has become. The Neanderthal is now a muscle-bound wrestler or a thug; the Hero, a forgotten corpse on some forgotten battlefield; the Sexual Athlete, a candidate for AIDS and herpes; the Superman, a panderer to those commercial interests that will pay the most to buy his name; the Dominance Drive, the producer of two-bit strongmen and kleptomaniacs who delight in the perversion of power; the Playboy, a Viagra consumer; the Provider, a pitiful workaholic. Feel free to further extrapolate. In short, what once was useful has now become a disabling sickness, an endemic pathology that has infested the social order with the tenacity of a virus. Viral infections are damnably difficult to eradicate even when properly diagnosed. How to proceed?

This will prove to be somewhat of a Herculean task for even the best-intentioned. An entity that has evolved over so many centuries, and has become so integrated into the trivia of everyday existence, will not be cavalierly dispensed with by some divine fiat or the wave of some judicial or legislative wand. Nevertheless, the moment of mobilization may have arrived, albeit unheralded by the blare of trumpets. It is difficult to go wrong quoting Shakespeare, who wrote:

> *There is a tide in the affairs of men,*
> *Which, taken at the flood, leads on to fortune;*
> *Omitted, all the voyage of their life*

Is bound in shallows and in miseries.
On such a full sea are we now afloat
We must take the current when it serves,
Or lose our ventures.

The tide is now, the flood is here, and the current begs to be taken. The role of the male in our contemporary society has reached that crucial juncture in which he may retire from the field, a wounded and defeated warrior, or summon up his considerable resources, modify the direction of social evolution by paying more attention to his rationality than to his previous social programming. A full-court press is called for. Begin with a public identification of a "problem"; which should come to be looked upon as an alien "something"; which is really a "public health menace"; which calls for the "mobilization" of a concerned citizenry; which will result in "serious" educational efforts by schools, all the media, and in public forums. A propaganda blitz, so to speak, with torrents of writings on the topic flooding Amazon.com, and sweeping Borders and Barnes & Noble up in the deluge. Even the stars of the "Superman Syndrome" may be enticed to lend their efforts to so worthy a cause, and to bask in the astral public relations bonanza that will ensue. Does this all have a familiar ring to it? It should. Similar approaches have been utilized by the women's movement, by the campaigns against cigarettes and guns, in the fight against AIDS, and in so many other causes as well, with varying degrees of success. This crusade, however, can have an even broader, deeper, and more urgent appeal. Not only does it directly impact the entire male half of our citizens, but it has profound effects on their wives, sweethearts, and daughters. They could well become the strongest of advocates. Successful campaigns have started with less.

At the outset, expect no bursts of impassioned applause, no hurrahs, bravos, or olés. Anticipate instead the grudging resistance, the silent avoidance, and the hostile gibe. Men, women, and their society have vast unconscious investments in the Mystique, and might understandably be expected to stoutly defend their perceived interests. It will take patience, perspiration, and perseverance to convince them that their investment is a misplaced and losing proposition.

Society, after all, thrives on the Achiever Complex as the hotspur of progress. It looks to the Dominance Drive for a steady supply of politicians, and to serve as the springboard for those with inclinations toward the accretion of power. It relies on the devotion and overexertion of the Provider to produce, to earn, and to borrow the wherewithal to keep the economy overheatedly rolling along with geometric progression. It requires the supermaniacal and heroic masculine ideal to provide the soldiery ready to risk life and limb in warfare, and to produce the spectacle of the male automaton for its panoply, parades, and panache. Indeed, so much of the social minutiae is ordered around the Mystique that its too sudden demise might be a shock, akin to a momentary transport to the land of Oz. Anticipate initial social antipathy.

The resistive male will hotly hold to his imagined prerogatives, to the myth of male superiority with its specter of power and glory. His fantasy of sexual athleticism, of playboy potentials, of the hero who is yet to be, will not readily surrender to such prosaic matters as mere survival. Expect no paeans from many penile possessors.

Some women may bemoan the ensuing lack of enthusiasm on the part of the Provider, mourn the loss of the Superman, and nostalgically yearn for those extra efforts of the Sexual Athlete. Those who bask in the reflected sun of the Achiever may lose a bit of their tan. Among women who relish an infantile role, the maturity and responsibility forced upon them by the dissolution of the Mystique will come as bitter medicine.

The most vocal opposition to the ousting of the Mystique will come from both male and female chauvinists. The male chauvinist has been sufficiently caricatured, blasphemed, and vilified, negating any undue influence that he may have possessed. His blatancy has made him a laughable character and perhaps deservedly so. Robert Bly, so to speak.

The female chauvinist is a different genus, however, and comes in two seemingly opposing species. The militant female chauvinist simply believes that she belongs to the superior sex, and loudly proclaims her conviction. The plight of the male is relatively inconsequential to her. She cares little about the Masculine Mystique, since she doesn't believe in it in the first place. As an illustration, read *The First Sex* by Helen E. Fisher (New York: Random House, 1999).

The other species of female chauvinist, the covert chauvinist, will be a far more subtle and serious antagonist. This species extols the difference between the sexes and demands that the cultural male and female stereotypes be stoutly maintained. Having thus become the philosophical bed

companion of the male chauvinist, she becomes the bo-
somed and vaginated instrument of the Masculine Mystique. Insisting on the validity of male superiority and
supremacy, she correspondingly demands the entire spectrum of female prerogatives predicated on the caricatured
weakness, passivity, and helplessness of the female. In her
exaltation of the Mystique, she impales the male, not only
as her everlasting Provider, Hero, and Achiever, but also
as her eternal servitor and supplicant. She can be recognized
by her posturing as the consummate female, by her eval-
uation of men solely in terms of their power and achievement, and by her obscene use of passivity. She demands
protection and genteel niceties, and rather than being sin-
cerely flattered by them, expects the male sacrifice as her
due, being "only a hapless female." Most psychiatrists have
seen her husband, desperate for a divorce, but guilt-ridden
beyond reason lest his fragile flower wilt and die should
they separate. Yet, after the divorce, she is amazingly adept
at quickly fastening on to another victim.

The covert female chauvinist emerges as a formidable
antagonist to the liberation and survival of the male, since
the entirety of her lifestyle is predicated on the maintenance
of the Masculine Mystique.

Apparently, the Mystique has its awesome array of defenders, numerous and diverse, highly invested and
strongly motivated. From the overall strategic standpoint,
the defenders must be made aware of the exorbitant price
the Mystique exacts from its devotees, a bizarre cost-benefit
ratio in which the price paid is far in excess of any benefits
conceivably derived.

Society as a whole pays the scathing price of a fragmented social order. The Mystique can be directly implicated as the prime or accessory agent behind warfare, with its limitless toll of human agony and social disruption, in governmental mismanagement, in the rise of vocational discontent, in the unconscionably high suicide and homicide rates, among other unimaginables. Every real red-blooded American male should be entitled to carry a six-shooter, shouldn't he? If he shoots sickly, aw shucks! An insufficiently appreciated horror of the Mystique is the rigidity its stereotypes impose upon the social corpus. Even a cognizant political personage, or an aware social reformer, experiences difficulty in breaking free from its coercive caricatures, i.e., if the Messiah actually descended from the heavens, but he was somewhat corpulent, rather short, and balding, who would believe him? Our saviors should be tall, thin, and rangy.

The sacrifice suffered by the male, were he to turn away from his love affair with the Mystique, is realistically negligible. Imitating a Satanic pact, which is of highly questionable legality, the Mystique has offered men fantasies and impossible ideals, in exchange for their souls and their humanity. In turning from the Mystique, the male will surrender only anachronistic and meaningless prerogatives. In rejoining the other half of the human race, he may more equitably share the responsibility and the workload with his female counterpart. His survival might be enhanced by greater affection and satisfaction from women, who may become more his companions than his antagonists.

College campuses throughout the United States have become inundated with courses in women's studies, a dive into the wellsprings of the female experience, with some universities offering it as a major area of study. Wittingly or not, "feminology" has been created as a new field within the social sciences. And this is good, personally and educationally, as is anything that broadens the depths of one's self-awareness and perception. Considering the tenuous state of the oppressed male, at least equal academic treatment is called for. The science of "hominology" or "masculinism" ought to be created and explored. New ideas ought to be injected into the varicosed veins of a society that often opts for the male status quo. "A Survey of Hominology" in academic clothes has its uses: it would legitimize, popularize, and focus in on the problem. It would attract bright young brains to fertilize the field, and it would produce federal grants, subsidies, and foundation backing, allowing more accurate information to be gathered in a shorter period of time, thus getting that poor chap off that vine that much sooner. Pecuniary power has been known to influence modifications of the public mind and mores. Imagine courses such as "The Male Image in Literature: From Ulysses to Leopold Bloom," or "Men, From an Anthropological Perspective," and "The Psychophysiology of the Male Member of Society." Academic plums, all. In fact, equal credit and time devoted to both men's and women's studies and even joint courses would enrich the lives of their participants immensely, and should be given serious consideration.

Women, Women, Women, Women...

The survival and the emancipation of the male involves not only the rejection of the Mystique, but the formation of alliances with the women in his life.

Previously, the point was made that when the Mystique's swan song is finally sung, women stand to gain the rational goals of the women's movement, plus a few additional bonuses. Fulfillment as independent human beings, with increased latitude for personal growth and development, would inevitably follow the establishment of a peer relationship with the male. Discrimination against the female by society has always been strongly encouraged and abetted by the Mystique. Its departure would remove an agent provocateur behind their subjugation. No longer inhibited from a free and equal relationship with their lovers and mates, the battle of the sexes might veer toward an unconditional truce. While this may not exactly return Adam and Eve to their Edenic idyll, it would be a step in the right direction. Women would benefit from the reduced intensity of male exertions as Provider, Achiever, and happy Hero by a diminution in premature death and disability of their husbands, with couples consequently living longer lives together, marked by less acrimony and greater conjugal activity.

However, men must first come to terms with the women's movement, and vice versa. The twenty-first century will probably witness a feminist tidal wave, with women gaining proportionally greater shares of the economic, vocational, and political pies. The movement has

already enjoyed success in three elemental areas: the acquisition of "rights," liberation from their perceived colo-
nial status, and the formation of organizations to advance
their agenda. Men, in the role of passive spectators, have
been unable to effectively recognize and deal with an
ephemeral force that is deconstructing much of their lives.
Their lack of cohesion and constructive confrontation has
allowed the WM to unopposedly go to extremes in some
areas. "Male bonding" has been a pathetically ineffective
instrument when confronting an organized feminist crusade. The inherent brittleness of the male psyche, coupled
with his inability to admit to the existence of so formidable
an "adversary" as "women," has left him individually and
organizationally impaired, but increased male activism is
obviously called for. Why, for example, should feminist
groups be allowed to indiscriminately inject their agenda
into college curricula, with so little objection from male
academicians? Should the fear of being judged "politically
incorrect" be a perpetual Sword of Damocles hanging over
male heads, or can the more courageous male rely on his
colleagues for support? Should not males cooperate in similar efforts? When ten-year-old kids are dismissed from
schools for "sexual harassment," which is little more than
boy-girl interplay, haven't things gone a bit far?

Of course women deserve a larger vocational role, but
should the male blithely abdicate so broadly when basic
needs are threatened, and without protest? These and so
many other problems arise. Are they better solved by gender warfare or by a Grand Alliance?

The WM is certainly more than just a group of
dissatisfied women with unconscious penis envy, over-

compensating for a sense of biological inferiority. The old adage that "anatomy is destiny" is only partially true. Many of their aims and activities reflect legitimate protests of an intelligent, determined, and articulate group of women. It has voiced authentic problems women encounter, not only within the American culture, but worldwide, e.g., genital mutilation, and safer and more available abortions. Parenthetically, can anyone doubt that if men became pregnant instead of women, free abortion would not only have been permitted, but sanctified, centuries ago. Additionally, more prosaic-sounding achievements such as the right to independent credit and property, and stronger stances in divorce courts have only been obtained after hard-fought battles.

However, the Yang-Yin archetype has been drastically extrapolated upon. The Manichean duality, the good gals versus the bad guys, has been so markedly overplayed that power transactions are perceived as the coin of the realm, to the exclusion of all else. In a world riven by inimical factions, too many discordant notes are injected. How much higher should the temperature of turmoil be raised? *Men Are From Mars, Women Are From Venus* is a cute title, but a silly thesis. We do inhabit the same planet. Should the male-female relationship be transmuted into an abattoir, or should we cry "Enough"?

This may be facilitated by the increasing awareness that the successes of the WM have opened it to the Law of Unintended Consequences. Increases in earnings have been associated with decreases in alimony grants; increased concerns about the appearance of even a whiff of sexual harassment have resulted in diminished privacy time between male professors and female students, and male supervisors with female associates, obliterating many all-important mentoring experiences. Disparities between the woman's accession to success in sharp contrast to the man's discouragement have resulted in many prematurely empty nests, to the satisfaction of no one. Bursts of feminine sexual "exuberance" have deflated otherwise ardent suitors. Additionally, there appears to be increased disillusionment among the "I can have it all" group of feminists, now in their late thirties, forties, and fifties, who have become more aware of the unforeseen prices they have and are presently paying. Future unintended consequences are still in the birthing stage. Those mentioned scrape the top of the iceberg.

In its latest stages, much of the WM has lost its cohesiveness, which may afford men increased opportunity to deal with its varied manifestations. In *The Whole Woman*, Germaine Greer in 1999 wrote a eulogy for the movement, whether intended or not: "It is because feminism is not egotistic that its force has been dissipated among a flotilla of other concerns, the peace movement, the green movement, gay liberation, black liberation, anti-pornography, animal rights, the ordination of women, HIV and AIDS. In every street demonstration, direct action, picket, whatever, you will see feminists coping the flack in the front line, though they will seldom be identified as spokespersons." Note the relative absence of male-female antagonisms, giving way to the broader human concerns. There does seem to be hope. Perhaps "feminism" will be replaced by "humanism" in a decade, or two, or three.

This matter of survival, the grist of male emancipation, would be incomplete without at least an italicized potpourri of particulars to be tucked away in the recesses of any male first-aid kits for more immediate use.

Let's not only dispense with the Mystique, but inoculate future generations against it. The successful survivor, like Sabatini's Scaramouche, should be born with the gift of laughter, and the sense that the world is mad. Since most men are not born with so beneficent a patrimony, it is incumbent upon them to develop it as rapidly as possible. The male neophyte should be informed that life has more than its share of absurdities and tribulations. Little boys as well as big men should be allowed to cry, to express and receive affection and tender feeling, to hug and kiss. Being naturally human is neither "weakening" nor criminal; the attempt to fashion a rod of steel from young human flesh is. De-emphasizing violence is long past due; our society is already supersaturated with its excesses. Children are being rewarded for aggressive behavior by parents who encourage winning at any cost. Tell them that "winning at any cost" costs, often too much. The heroic ideals offered to our offspring are generally victors in violence. How often are children told that most heroic deeds, in fact, arise, not from choice, but instead are impelled by the push of circumstances? How many of our heroes were actually and knowingly ready to voluntarily "lay down their lives" for any cause? Of course, heroes deserve respect, but they merit our understanding as well. Braving the odds can be commendable, suicide is suspect. Our military and historical heroes, the protagonists of movies and television series, and even the gods taught in mythology classes frequently excel in manufactured murder and mayhem. Apparently, the human race has fewer built-in inhibitions against killing members of its own species than any other mammal, with the possible exception of the rat. If we continue to reward and idealize aggression and violence, we only encourage and abet a rat-pack mentality, which can eventually shorten the survival not only of the male, but of the entire human race. Children should be informed that "legitimate self-assertion," the reasonable expression of one's own person or territory, is their inalienable right, but that aggression, the forceful intrusion into the rights of others, is a tool only to be used with careful deliberation.

Let's keep the Neanderthal properly confined, preferably in a gilded cage, or make his modern expression a joke and an object of derision. Under the proper circumstances and appropriately applied, humor can be lethal to the fallacious and the fraudulent. Our new masculine heroes should be those who can rise above the conventional, who view the manifestations of the Mystique, not with contempt, but with pity and understanding, as relics of the past.

The Achiever Complex should be equated with Santayana's definition of fanaticism: "Redoubling your effort when you have forgotten your aim." The man obsessed with achievement should have a reasonable goal in mind. Once this goal is attained, a thoughtful and reflective pause is in order. If he feels impelled to further push on, with no apparent end in view, he should calculate the personal costs involved, and perhaps seek a psychiatric consultation if the price outweighs any reasonable and expectable benefits.

The Sexual Athlete should take a seventh-inning stretch and consider the welfare of his penis. While an increase in the recreational aspects of sex is strongly recommended, the relational components should not be negated. "The Sex Life of a Penis" is not to be construed as an invitation to a never-ending and indiscriminate orgy. In their proper proportion and place, relational considerations enhance sexual satisfaction. A sexual experience should be appreciated, like a fine wine, rather than being regarded as a chore, a test, or an act completely devoid of significance. Chaotic or indiscriminate sexuality is a rather dubious delight. A man related the following incident: "I was dining alone at a restaurant. An attractive woman sat at an adjacent table. Naturally, I smiled at her, and was rather pleasantly surprised when she smiled back. I invited her to join me, and she happily obliged. You can imagine my embarrassment when she reminded me that we had slept together only six months ago." Something is clearly out of whack here. There is nothing sacred or holy about sex, but there is something intimate and personal in sex.

Despite the differences in the physiological sexual capacities and responses of men and women, there exists a rough equality in their sexualities. Women should recognize the latent fragility of many men, encourage rather than reject, and by judicious behavior, salvage difficult but potentially rewarding relationships. On the other hand, a "man's man" will imagine himself in his partner's place, inquire what turns her on and off, and oblige, throwing stereotyped notions to the wind. If she is more apt to "come" using lingual, manual, or vibratory stimuli, great. The clitoris should be given as much respect and latitude as the penis. It is *no*, repeat, *no*, negative reflection on someone's masculinity. Each woman has her own particular orgastic physiological responses. The happily satisfied woman is more apt to have a happily satisfied partner, and satisfaction may not necessarily be intertwined with an orgasm. It is also helpful to remember that a single sexual performance is not necessarily a barometer of ability, affection, or concern; it may only be an expression of anxiety, alcohol, or fatigue.

Moving from the more direct expressions of the Mystique to other pressing problems of male survival, the question of lifestyle and philosophical outlook must be considered by the emancipated male.

Man's wonderful workaday world apparently falls short of the ecstatic. The Provider can end up as little more than a beast of burden, for whom life and work are synonymous. This cries out for modification. A man is more than that which he produces or the corporate title on his business card; and his vocation should consequently be only a circumscribed area within the totality of his identity. A robotic, though financially remunerative, career often makes for a colorless and pointless existence. The puritan work ethic should be removed as the Eleventh Commandment. If a man provides for himself and his family, he is worthy of honor. If he goes beyond, and devotes his life to his work, well, that's his option or his problem, but he deserves no automatic chorus of accolades as a reward. Industry has finally taken notice of vocational discontent, particularly since unemployment is at a low ebb. It is timely then to insist upon more respect, responsibility, and autonomy at work. Pushing medical residents and associates at legal firms to put in eighty- and ninety-hour work weeks, to the destruction of their social and marital lives, for example, is both brutal and unnecessary. I have treated a number of these talented people, forced to choose between living a decent life, and literally sacrificing their youth for a potential place in the sun. This is more an adolescent rite of passage, demanded by those in power who should know better. It's time for them to grow up. Job descriptions can be redesigned to enhance the worker's dignity, and to deliberately allow for more creative opportunities. Furthermore, the postretirement depression must be anticipated, and management should provide sufficient preparation for it, perhaps as a major function of the human resources departments. Management owes this debt to its employees; there are obligations that do extend beyond the bottom line. Don't just leave it to the psychiatrists to pick up the pieces. Benjamin Disraeli commented: "Youth is a blunder, manhood a struggle, and old age a regret." Obviously we cannot totally remove remorsefulness from the elderly, but we can modify the vocational component in it.

Marriage and family should be freed from society's social imperatives. A man should regard marriage as one of several lifestyles that he is free to choose or avoid, devoid of social stigma or disapprobation, depending only on one's personal proclivities. A man should only marry if he is reasonably comfortable with the idea, and with his prospective spouse. Divorce is emotionally wrenching and financially devastating. A wife should be selected with commonality and compatibility given as much weight as the romantic factor. From its inception, a marriage should hopefully be viewed as a lifelong relationship, which should be constantly worked at, with a continual sharing of responsibilities and interests. Children should be regarded as luxuries rather than necessities. By all means conceive them, but only if both partners are willing to make the requisite investment in affection, time, and money. The seventeenth-century Deists postulated a God who created the world, and then left it to spin on its own. One simply cannot do this with children. Once they are created, they require the continuing involvement of both parents, very definitely including the interest and concern of their father. If he is not prepared for so extensive an undertaking, he may be left with a pack of severely troubled children who can prove to be a plague rather than a source of perpetual pleasure. Think twice, or a third time, before you make that final insemination.

While I heartily endorse the legalization of "domestic partnerships" with all their attendant benefits, the legitimization of same-sex unions under the rubric of "marriage" troubles me. Man-woman "marriage," with, or even without children, presently remains the bedrock of an otherwise increasingly plasticized and depersonalized social order. If this concept, with all its evident problems, be further diluted by same-sex, or ménage-à-trois, or group "marriages" in the near future, the word will have lost its meaning, and our social order will have lost a major keystone. "Those friends thou hast / and their adoption tried / Grapple them to thy soul with hoops of steel," sayeth the Bard, and the institution of marriage has been one of civilization's best friends.

New modifications of the perceived essence of masculinity must be developed, which are based on the physiology and neural constructions of the male, rather than grounded in either archaic forms or current political exigencies and political correctness. These constructs, outlined

Harvey E. Kaye, M.D.

in more detail in chapter 2, "The Male in the Masculinity Maze," should sharpen the male image, rather than soften it. It should be recognized that there are genuine gender differences, previously discussed, that naturally lead to complementary differences in social roles and career paths, without the necessity of all-out gender warfare. Men, for example, are more action-prone while women are more relationship-prone; men are physically stronger, while women communicate better and are less warlike. Let women organize, and let men act. Ergo, divest ourselves of notions of numerical equality in each and every area, even allowing women to more pacifically govern, while the men be the risk-taking venture capitalists, the firefighters, or the unfettered backbone of our defense forces. All that "differs" is not necessarily "bias"; there is no need for every professional football squad to consist of eleven women and eleven men. Competition between sexes should give way to reasonable accommodation. The grotesqueries of the Mystique should, of course, be discarded, with reasonable allowances made for the retention of in-bred male propensities toward reasonable risk-taking, to the occasional swagger, to sensible egotism and territoriality, to the realities of the male makeup in contrast to a gargoyle.

The fundamental item in a survival kit: a man is first a human being, his maleness or masculinity being only a secondary phenomenon. The emphasis should always devolve on his humanness, with "masculinity" far back in second or third place. As a male his potentials are great, but so is his vulnerability. There is a joy in mastery and creativity, but there is also joy in living a full and satisfactory life, one which, if given the chance, the man would elect to repeat.

The liberation of the male has within it echoes of the Promethean legend. The Titan, Prometheus, was condemned by Zeus to be chained to a rock, with a vulture constantly gnawing away at his heart, for defying the gods by stealing fire (knowledge?) from the heavens, and teaching its secrets to men. What would men be like once they have been unchained, and all the creativity and feelings that have been bound up by the Mystique are freed?

There is a continuum between Camus's "Man must live and create. Live to the point of tears," and Euripides' "Life is a short affair. We should make it smooth and free of strife." Each man must find the point between these polarities that best suits his constitution and psychology, and stick to it, despite the pushing and the prodding of even the best-intentioned souls within his environmental orbit. It is written that the Buddha's final words to his disciples were: "Seek thy salvation with diligence." What more can man do?